Leone

"Dan values family very highly. A lot of the respect that he has on a personal level carries forward in business....Everyone needs someone to talk to, and I trusted him implicitly."

— L. Douglas Wilder, former Virginia governor.

"I liked that Dan wasn't stuck-up. He wasn't one of those people. He was a man of integrity, a man of his word....You can't confide in everyone, but I could confide in him."

— Bruce Smith, former defensive end for the Washington Redskins and Buffalo Bills and NFL Hall of Fame inductee.

2/2/15

Dedicated to my loving parents,
Alfred and Sarah.

Your love, guidance and support
gave me the confidence to succeed.

From the Ground Up
by Dan Hoffler
with Joe Coccaro

Edited by Cheryl Ross
Cover and text designed by John Köehler

ISBN 9781938467448

For more information about this book and all other inquiries,
please contact John Koehler, john@koehlerbooks.com 757-289-6006
210 60th Street, Virginia Beach, Virginia 23451

Published by

koehlerbooks
an imprint of Morgan James Publishing

5 Penn Plaza, 23rd floor
c/o Morgan James Publishing
New York, NY 10001
212-574-7939
www.koehlerbooks.com

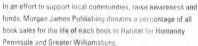

In an effort to support local communities, raise awareness and funds, Morgan James Publishing donates a percentage of all book sales for the life of each book to Habitat for Humanity Peninsula and Greater Williamsburg.
Get involved today, visit www.MorganJamesBuilds.com

Dan Hoffler

WITH JOE COCCARO

From the Ground Up

NEW YORK

VIRGINIA

Introduction

Dad wanted to show me where he worked. Until now, his job had been somewhat of a mystery. I remember Mom dropping off Dad at work on occasion. I'd be in the car, gazing at the shipyard and thinking that it looked endless. Massive ships in dry dock on the water's edge with their great hulls were taller than any building I had ever seen. Some had big white numbers, meaning they were warships.

Parking lots the size of football fields were packed with pick-ups and Chevys. Workers changing shifts filed in and out of the entrance gates like bees to a hive in the spring.

Dad stood out from most men entering and exiting. He wore a white shirt and tie, a fact my mother was always proud of. Dad was a draftsman, an office worker. Most others were welders, pipefitters, electricians, laborers, painters or sandblasters. They donned overalls or jeans, sweatshirts and ball caps. They had beards, rough hands, smoked cigarettes, ate ham sandwiches and drank coffee from a thermos. The tint of their work clothes was much like the shipyard itself: lots of dark blues, grays and browns. Nowhere was Portsmouth, Virginia's lineage as a blue-collar town more apparent.

It was on a Saturday morning after breakfast that Dad took me for "the visit." I was about age five.

I stood a few steps behind Dad as we approached an entrance gate. Dad spoke briefly and quietly to a security guard. I don't remember exactly what the man said to my father, but I am clear about the way Dad was treated.

My dad, Alfred Hoffler, was then as he always has been, gentle and soft-spoken, with soft blue eyes and an easy smile. Not once as a boy or later in life did my father raise his voice at me, my sister, and certainly not my mother, Sarah. He rarely showed disappointment or frustration and never displayed anger. He showed the same restraint and civility on the morning of our visit to the shipyard.

The guard was smug and condescending. He clearly didn't want to let us into the yard. I remember my father being embarrassed, saying only that he wanted to show his son where he worked, that we wouldn't be roaming around the yard itself, only his office. Others had been allowed to bring kin to work.

The guard insulted my father and, even worse, marginalized a man in front of his son. He made my father grovel for no apparent reason other than to demonstrate his own authority. My father was not so important that the guard would just let him enter unquestioned. The guard could, if he wanted, turn my father away.

I remained silent, trying at first to understand what was happening, and then, why. Anger came next and then a lesson that imprinted me forever. I decided at that moment that I never wanted to be treated with such disrespect; I never wanted to be so beholden to another person or job that a boss, coworker or security guard could humiliate me without consequence. I never wanted to be that callous or insensitive to others, seeing the hurt on my dad's face. For me, the revelation was about showing decency to others and expecting the same in return. Never since that day have I seen the upside in being disrespectful or demeaning—to anyone. After our visit that day, I left determined that no one would douse my self-esteem.

My father's temperament and my mother's unrelenting encouragement provided the foundation for my life as a father businessman and adventurer. I owe them everything, and perhaps more importantly, I admire them deeply. They are my heroes.

There were no silver spoons in my young life, but there were lots of silver linings. Alfred and Sarah Hoffler taught me to believe in myself, not settle for less, and to aim high. I listened to them, and because of their lessons things usually turned out well for me, even if they started off shaky. I am not sure what to call it—fate, luck, karma, divine intervention? More than once I have made spontaneous decisions for reasons I still do not fully understand. These choices either enabled me to avert financial disaster or to profit tremendously. In business, timing isn't everything, but it can be hugely important. I have also been a student of human behavior. My mentor, a Texas oilman named Jim Fisher, taught me to "trust my gut." That's been especially important when sorting out whom to do business with.

I decided to chronicle my life's journey with the hope that my family, supporters, coworkers and others will learn from my fits and starts. I hope to inspire others who come from common backgrounds such as mine. I hope my story shows that if you believe in yourself, others will believe in you. As for those who do not, forget about them. I have found most of my detractors to be envious, petty or political.

This book is also a tribute to my parents and the core group of partners and friends who believed in me and remained loyal through three recessions, three marriages, a few mistakes and some bad press. My wife, Valerie, and my children have also been loving and stable forces in my life.

I have been fortunate, more fortunate than most, to have such dedicated partners and family to lean on. My deepest gratitude goes to my lifelong friend and right-hand man, Russ Kirk, and the gifted executive who runs the day-to-day affairs of our development and construction businesses, Louis Haddad. With these men at the helm, my company, Armada Hoffler, has built some of the grandest hotels, office buildings and industrial parks on the East Coast. Our buildings fill the skylines of Virginia Beach, Norfolk, Washington and Baltimore. When I see these trophies in the sky, I think of Russ, Lou and the dedicated staff who helped shape Armada Hoffler over three decades.

Through our dealings I have come to know others with money and influence. Friends include CEOs of Fortune 500 companies, NASCAR drivers, NFL stars, U.S. senators, mayors, Virginia governors, Navy admirals and famous entertainers. Successful people often travel the same orbits. It's natural that they form bonds that sometimes sprout into friendships. Deals do get made over drinks, private dinners and while on exotic trips. But they're initiated on trust and built upon a bedrock of integrity.

Among those dearest to me are people most like my parents, honest folks with average incomes toiling to be providers and to do right by others. I often find "regular" people—some of them farmers, tradesmen, secretaries, hunting guides, real estate agents and restaurant staffers—even more extraordinary than those with big titles and several homes. Integrity, I have found, is a common denominator for success in all of us. People without it are often not true to themselves, which makes it impossible to be true to others. Avoid them in business and in life.

You'll find in these pages that I don't pretend to be some

kind of business apostle or moralist or tech-savvy trailblazer. My success has come from the tried-and-true formula of hard work and salesmanship. I am a "people" guy, an extrovert who likes getting to know folks and being around others who enjoy life. I see the possibilities in people and business deals and try to match the two. You might say I am a capitalistic Cupid.

When you do as many deals as I have, compete against others with big egos and befriend high-profile politicians, you're bound to get bruised and make some mistakes. I have a list of regrets, as most people do. I have been divorced twice; I have had some failed investments; I have been vindictive more than once; I can be impatient. Some politicians don't like me, and I do have business competitors who root against me. On the flip side, I have enjoyed tailored suits, imported cars, big boats, world travel and lots of houses with furnishings from around the world. Call me flamboyant; I'll accept that. I like having fun with my money, and I like my friends and family to enjoy it too. I buy expensive things because I never had them growing up—not just to show off. After all of these years, I am still a Portsmouth kid who likes Miller Lite, fried chicken, joking with friends, flirting with women and being outdoors.

Taxidermists love me, that's for sure. I have hunted and fished on five continents and have a roomful of mounted trophies. They include a white rhino that charged me in Africa, a ten-foot polar bear from the Arctic Circle, Himalayan tahr from New Zealand, a leopard from Africa, waterfowl from Argentina, killer fish from the Amazon, mountain sheep from ten thousand feet up the Canadian Rockies, grizzly bears from Russia, grouse from European estates, and whitetails and fox from my beloved Eastern Shore of Virginia. I make no apologies to those offended by hunting and fishing. It's a passion that runs deep, planted early in life and intensifying with age. I made a fortune creating buildings and working indoors. I have spent a fortune exploring the outdoors at some of the most remote regions on the globe.

My hunting exploits have taught me a lot about conservation. Most people don't realize how the two go hand in hand. Hunting lands have become increasingly pressured by development and poaching, prompting land owners and governments to collaborate to protect wildlife and the land it lives on. Entire species that had nearly been extinct have rebounded because of these efforts, especially in Africa.

It's also been very important to me that the animals I have taken in the field do not go to waste. I'll never forget the scene outside of a small village in Zimbabwe. We took an old bull elephant that hunting preserve managers wanted culled from the herd. The word quickly spread and seventy—I counted them—villagers swarmed the carcass. Adults with machetes carved up every bit of that animal for food, and children hauled away the meat in flour sacks. Within eight hours, the bones were stripped clean. Villagers celebrated that night.

My enthusiasm for conservation and hunting landed me on the board of the Virginia Department of Game and Inland Fisheries. I was proud to serve as chairman and determined to improve the pay and morale of the game wardens who risk their lives enforcing hunting and fishing laws. A series of administrative missteps and, I am convinced, viciousness from political adversaries prompted me to step down from the board. I learned just how damaging the disconnect between perception and truth can be. In an odd way, I have gained even more respect for public officials, who endure the constant scrutiny of critics and foes. Those in the spotlight rarely are forgiven—or thanked.

Since childhood I have been a glass-is-half-full person. I don't allow shortcomings or disappointments to overshadow joy and success or slow my momentum. I focus on what can be accomplished—not what is unattainable. I have learned that the "impossible" only takes longer. I have not allowed others to define me or of what I am capable. My personal journey has been guided by people with big hearts and big minds. I have tried to learn from their successes and failures and to always keep life's ebbs and flows in perspective. There are no straight lines in life. Success comes with setbacks. Two steps forward, one step back. What's most important is how you deal with both. I want my daughters, Sara and Kristy, and sons, Daniel and Hunter, and the generations of my family to come, to know my journey and to learn from it. My legacy to them, I hope, will be more than a trust fund or the Hoffler name on buildings. I also hope that this book stokes the confidence of other "regular" people who want to make a mark of their own. If life's lessons can be distilled into a short list, here is mine:

Believe in yourself.

Do the right thing.

Don't give up.

Be honorable.

Never compromise your integrity.

Laugh and have fun.

In the quiet moments, while waiting for first light in a duck blind, traveling on a plane to a corporate board meeting or enjoying a beer while looking out over the Chesapeake Bay from my Eastern Shore farm, I think about my parents, my journey, my business partners and my closest friends. I feel blessed to have had so many who care about me and with whom to share my good fortune. I know that things could have turned out very differently for me if not for the example of my mother and father. They taught me to see the good in others and in myself.

Chapter I
Sarah

*"From a young age, Mother tried to instill confidence.
She believed I could achieve."*

My mother wished she had been Irish. She never said exactly why except that she liked the ring of Irish names and music. That's why she named me Daniel and why she always referred to me as Danny.

Mom's accent strongly suggests her Southern roots. Many have told me that I get my accent, and what temper I have, from her. Mother's is a polished lilt, lighter than the thick drawl of southern Appalachia, but nonetheless pronounced. Her mannerisms match her voice: elegant but direct. She has always shown displeasure without being harsh or critical. A tense stare from her steely eyes make her feelings abundantly clear. She isn't one to show too much zeal, except when it comes to defending or protecting her kids. I always thought Mom would have made a great poker player.

Mother was the third of twelve children born to Vines Collier and Jennie Weatherby. There were four girls and eight boys. One of the boys died as an infant. With that many kids, Vines insisted on lots of structure in the household. The Collier gaggle walked three miles to Sunday school and largely played among themselves on the family farm. The mail was delivered just once a week. Education was important to Vines, who insisted that all of his children graduate from high school. He loved to read and instilled a sense of learning in his offspring.

Sarah Collier was born on April 26, 1924, in the farmhouse where she was raised. So were most of her brothers and sisters. Vines didn't have much money, so he would barter for doctor's services. Payments could be a sack of flour from his general store or a cord of firewood. A gallon of milk back then cost about fifty cents and average annual income in the country was about thirteen hundred dollars. Automobiles were still an extravagance in rural Georgia but increasing numbers of people were paying upward of three hundred dollars for one. That price was out of reach for Vines Collier's large family. Sarah would be embarrassed when dropped off at the one-room school by her father's horse-drawn buggy. Horses were cheap then and still populated Georgia country roads.

Much of the food served at dinner was either grown or butchered on the farm. The family sat together nearly every evening for dinner. There wasn't much discussion. Vines insisted on a quiet, civil meal. He might share some information at the dinner table that he heard while at the store, or he might quiz the children on school studies. The children, however, spoke only when spoken to. Mother remembers her dad as a kind and considerate man, but a father who very much ruled his domain.

If Vines or Jennie ever had a cross word the children were not witnesses. Conversation was polite and always civil. Disagreements were handled quietly and out of earshot. Collier children were disciplined for acting out or being disobedient, but punishment was mild. Sarah and her sisters were never spanked. Vines could be more stern, but never violent, with the boys.

The Collier farmhouse was modest. Many of the children shared bedrooms and slept on wooden bunks. Sarah remembers being in bed and staring through slight cracks in the ceiling into the starlit evening sky.

Descendants from both sides of my mother's family were English. The Colliers were among the first Europeans to colonize Yorktown, Virginia. Genealogical records date the family to 1583 from Darlaston in the County of Staffordshire. The English spelling of the name is Collyer, which was changed to Collier on American immigration records. Weatherby is an English name as well, although not as much is known about my great-grandmother's ancestry. The family's roots trace to Baltimore and Boston.

The Collier family dispersed, mostly to follow work opportunities. My mother's grandfather was a railroad worker who in the late 1800s was transferred to Georgia. The family settled in Manchester, a rural town east of Macon and about sixty miles or so north of Atlanta.

The Collier men had quick success in business and politics. In many ways they were the ruling family of nine-square-mile Warm Springs and neighboring Manchester. The Collier men were a tall, blue-eyed lot, well-known and highly regarded. My mother would often say that if someone wanted to get anything done in Manchester, they needed to speak with a Collier.

Vines Collier owned a general store and worked the family farm. One brother was a sheriff and his father was chief of police. Family members owned lots of land, selling timber from their farms and parlaying profits into more land. Some of that property is still in our family. Their crops were mostly cotton, which was processed at a local cotton gin. When mother got older, her parents sternly warned that she was not allowed to date anyone working at the cotton gin. She would have to do better.

There weren't many choices back then. Atlanta was still a small town, at least by current standards, and Georgia was still very much a farm culture healing from the ravages of the Civil War. Travel was limited, so many of the locals would wind up marrying someone from a neighboring farm. That would be the case with my mother. A neighboring childhood sweetheart would win her hand.

Sharecroppers—descendants of slaves—remained on the Collier farm, growing vegetables, cotton and grains and residing in houses on the property. Mother became an adjunct to one sharecropper family. She played with the children and would often sit on the lap of adult women who sang gospel songs and told stories as they rocked in chairs on the porch. Mother often shared meals with them or hung around their kitchen when pies were in the oven. It was an escape from her sometimes taunting brothers. Sarah was obviously aware that the black sharecroppers were treated differently from whites and that they lived more modestly, but she viewed them as extended family and the social structure of the still segregated South as a normal part of life.

Tragedy hit the family in 1927 when Vines died from a blood infection. It had been a fairly rapid illness, Mother recalls. Penicillin, which likely would have saved thirty-nine-year-old Vines, would be discovered one year later. Vines had been well-regarded locally as was evident from the turnout at his funeral. White friends and family members packed the church while dozens of blacks, who were not allowed inside, lined the road in tribute during the funeral procession. One black family sang a song they had written for Vines.

It was another illness that put my mother's hometown of Warm Springs on the map. The polio-stricken governor of New York, who would become the thirty-second president of the United States, had heard about a Georgia resort. It was built at an old fish hatchery in the late 1800s and it had healing powers. A spring running from Pine Mountain yielded mineral-rich water with temperatures an almost constant eighty-eight degrees.

Franklin D. Roosevelt first arrived at Warm Springs in 1924, nine years before he would be elected to the first of his four terms as president. He had hoped that bathing and exercising in the mineral water would strengthen his legs, which were nearly paralyzed by the disease. In a 2005 television movie about Roosevelt's life at Warm Springs, the president is seen wading in a pool at the resort with other patients and children. My mother would have been one of those children in real life.

In the movie, Roosevelt asked for the "Collier boys" at the train station on his first trip to Warm Springs. In real life, those Colliers he summoned were my mother's uncles. Sarah remembers subsequent visits by FDR. There weren't many automobiles that passed by my mother's house back then, and when one approached, it could be heard from a long way off, chugging or backfiring. Mother and her siblings would gather by the roadside and excitedly wave as FDR passed by on his way to the resort. He would wave back and flash his classic smile, sometimes with a cigarette on a stem dangling from his mouth while he tipped his hat.

Local children knew those who operated the spa and were allowed to swim in the mineral pool alongside patients. Mother remembers wading just a few feet from the president. He was friendly and cheerful, playfully splashing water at the children or tossing a ball.

The president visited so often that he built a six-room cottage near the resort. He named it the Little White House. Historians say he crafted portions of his New Deal while residing there. Roosevelt's legacy remains branded in and around Warm Springs, with a local airport, highway and state park bearing his name. My mother always held the president in high regard, even though she had general disregard for Democrats later in life.

Sarah graduated in 1940 and married a local fellow named David Perrins Boggs a year later. She called him Perrins. He did not work in a cotton gin. Perrins lived two farms away and met Sarah when they were very young. She and Perrins played together and attended the same school. The Boggs family was old Georgia of conservative Christian values. He was smart and respectful and well known to Vines and Jennie Collier.

Perrins and Sarah's union would be happy but brief. Perrins joined the fight against the Germans as a gunner on a B-24 Liberator, an Air Force bomber. He was stationed at a base near Charleston, South Carolina, where my mother joined him. She was pregnant when Perrins was deployed.

Sarah did not want to be alone with her infant, David, while her husband was away. Charleston was unfamiliar to her, so she headed north and moved in with her mother, Jennie, who had since relocated to Portsmouth, Virginia, after Vines's unexpected death.

Without her husband, Jennie could not keep the farm running and profitable. Her in-laws and other members of the Boggs family were unwilling to help support Jennie and her children. Some had looked down on her and Vines because they had so many children. They should have shown more self-restraint. Jennie was also not favored by the Boggs clan because her family, the Weatherbys, descended from the northern cities of Baltimore and Boston and was, therefore, Yankee.

Sarah and her young son moved in with Jennie and her gaggle of children, the youngest of who was age three. They packed into a row house on Elm Street, a neighborhood not far from the large naval shipyard. Sarah took a job in the shipyard and her brothers and sisters help watched her young son, David.

Perrins's combat missions, like so many during the war, were kept secret, so he couldn't reveal much in letters or phone calls to his wife. It wasn't unusual for Sarah not to hear from her husband for long stretches. After no word for a few months, Sarah became worried.

The Air Force never fully disclosed how Perrins and the B-24 crew died, probably because it's still a mystery. What mother did learn is that her husband's plane was over the Atlantic when it vanished in the area that has come to be known as the treacherous Bermuda Triangle. Some have speculated that the plane ran out of gas after the pilot mistakenly dumped his fuel. Others say it went down in a storm. Either way, the plane and its crew had simply vanished and were never found.

Mother received a message in March 1945 that her husband was missing. Six months later, David Perrins Boggs was declared dead. Moving in with her mother had proved to be fortuitous. Sarah didn't like Portsmouth but was grateful for the support of her family.

Chapter II
Alfred

"I have never had a cross word with my father.
People don't believe it, but it's true."

In the 1800s,three brothers crossed the Atlantic chasing the American dream. They were common German workmen looking for opportunity during a depressed time in Europe. The ship they boarded never quite made it to its destination. As the story goes, it wrecked just off the Outer Banks coast of North Carolina.

The three Hoffler men survived, presumably in lifeboats that got them to shore. Once on land, each chose a different path toward prosperity. One brother trekked inland and settled in nearby Gates County, which borders Virginia and to this day is still largely undeveloped farmland. The second brother set out for the West, possibly in search of gold or to homestead. He was never again heard from. The third brother wandered slightly north and settled in the area where the Chesapeake Bay, James

River and other tributaries converge, the place where the first English colony was established—the area known as Hampton Roads.

Portsmouth, Virginia, was bustling back then. The Navy had a huge presence, spawning ship building and repair work on the Elizabeth River, which connects with the James.

Alfred Judson Hoffler, my grandfather, worked on that shoreline. He was an athletic man and he preferred the outdoors, a trait I inherited and passed on to my sons. He was born in 1890 and as a young guy he played baseball professionally, earning at his peak seventy dollars a week as a pitcher. He supposedly had a wicked curveball that "he could make dance," according to my dad. The Cincinnati Reds must have thought so because they offered him a Major League contract.

Grandfather didn't want to uproot his family or leave them behind to pursue his big-league dream, so he remained in Portsmouth working as a carpenter and signing on as a mate for cargo ships that ran between Baltimore and Hampton Roads.

My grandfather married Louise A. Colb, a Baltimore born-and-raised gal of some sophistication who told everyone she was a few years younger than her husband. That would be a deception she took to her grave in 1951. Louise was actually ten years older than Alfred Sr. She lived the deception because society back then frowned upon older women marrying younger men.

Louise's father had been a glassblower in Germany, and she was a first-generation American. Growing up, my dad became accustomed to hearing German spoken at home by his mother. Louise worked on her English skills, attending the local Peabody Institute. She also loved to bake, filling their modest home with the smell of her pies and cookies and strudel. Dinner was another matter. Louise could bake but apparently she was a lousy cook. It was a standing joke in the house, but neither my dad nor his sister, Eleanor, complained.

Grandfather returned to the land of his ancestors as an American soldier in World War I. He was injured in battle but survived and returned to Portsmouth. Any hopes of playing baseball again vanished with the wounds. Sections of Portsmouth were thick with people like my grandfather after the war, newly arrived expatriates from Europe and first-generation Americans returning from combat. Alfred recalls his early years, living in a neighborhood called Prentis Park, surrounded by aunts and other family in row houses separated by only a few feet. Neighbors would often chat through open windows and hand, back and forth, items they borrowed from each other. It was a classic urban setting: families sharing meals; cousins, brothers and sisters running from house to house; men sharing rides to work; women with broken accents staying home raising children.

The Great Depression hit my family's father hard, as it did so many of the working class. Frugality was not an option. My father's family bought just the necessities and took work where it could be found. In the midst of those harsh years, in 1937, Alfred Sr. died of a heart attack at age forty-nine. My father helped fill the void by splitting his time between school and making money. Each weekday morning he would attend high school classes and each afternoon, work a job for four hours.

One of my father's relatives, a carpenter, helped Alfred land an apprenticeship with George T. McClain, a Portsmouth building supply store. One of the men there cottoned to my dad, encouraging young Alfred to draw plans for home builders buying supplies from the store. My father was a quick study and was soon earning twelve dollars a week sketching house designs and drafting blueprints.

Alfred graduated from Woodrow Wilson High School in 1939, excelling at geometry and science. His uncle Johnny helped set my father's path by encouraging him to become a government draftsman. My father first would have to pass a drafting test and then be invited into an apprentice program. Father took the test with an ink pen. That meant no margin for error, no eraser marks. My father is a resilient man not easily frazzled; because of that, he can focus. He did so on that particular test day.

Father was hired by the Norfolk Naval Shipyard in Portsmouth, which had exponentially expanded to supply the United States with warships. Portsmouth's potential for shipbuilding and maritime trade had been recognized as far back as 1620 by English colonialists. The emerging U.S. Navy recognized the potential too and purchased the Gosport Navy Shipyard, a large private shipbuilder founded in 1767. The yard, burned and destroyed by the Union Army during the Civil War, resurrected years later as Norfolk Naval Shipyard.

The historic yard became the economic engine that powered Portsmouth's economy. During World War II, it doubled in physical size on the banks of the Elizabeth River and more than tripled its workforce to forty-three thousand. The city's population swelled in tandem, exploding from fifty thousand residents to eighty thousand between 1940 and 1950. My father was part of that crest.

Alfred was assigned to the rigging and fitting group, working ten hours a day and often on weekends. He would help invent a pulley system that became vital on cargo ships. Skilled shipbuilders were in such demand that they received military service deferments during much of the war. That changed in 1944 for Alfred, who was drafted into the Army at age twenty-three and sent to London. Alfred was assigned to the 10th Armored Division, part of Gen. George S. Patton's Third Army. Someone in the Army must have figured that Dad's aptitude for design could be better spent keeping Patton's tanks and half-tracks rolling on land.

Dad carried an M-1 rifle or machine gun, often riding on the massive steel hulks or walking beside them. He was part of Patton's historic march that hunted down the Germans during their retreat from France. The war had wound down quickly after Patton's campaign and talk of its end was imminent. On April 2, 1945, less than a month before the Germans surrendered, Alfred was nearly killed.

Father's outfit had rumbled through Germany and was closing in on the Bavarian Alps, which were still being defended by Hitler's Third Reich. A German bazooka shell ricocheted off of a tank, gouging the road being traveled by the Americans and spraying shrapnel. Metal fragments ripped into Alfred's upper chest, hurling him into the air. His left leg snapped at the knee. Colleagues ran to a nearby village for medical help. An Army ambulance entered the fray, rescuing my father and two other wounded soldiers.

German machine guns fired on the Army ambulance. Bullets passed through the cab where the wounded lay. The ambulance driver steered off the road and through a cornfield to escape the barrage. My father remembers lurching and bouncing in the back and bullets hitting the truck. He remembers making it to the village and medics cutting off his left boot to evaluate his wounds. He was thankful for the morphine injections. Remarkably, my father lived. Even more astounding is that he was able to walk again. He returned to Portsmouth a war hero, donning a Bronze Star and crutches. He also returned to an empty home.

Chapter III
Beginnings

"My parents have been in love their whole lives.
In this day and age, that's almost unheard of.
It's a true love story."

Before my father had deployed, he met a young, attractive woman from Washington, D.C. He married the gal and enjoyed a short time with her. He returned from Europe to find that his young bride had vanished. He tracked her down back in Washington where she was sharing an apartment with another man. Father was disappointed by a love he thought was real but obviously wasn't. He was more embarrassed than angry. Soon afterward, he and the young woman mutually divorced.

Dad doesn't like discussing this brief marriage, and I never heard him speak unkindly about that woman. Alfred says only that they were very young and that she ultimately wanted to live a different kind of life. My mother has been less generous when describing Alfred's first wife.

Alfred hobbled for months on crutches to give his leg time to strengthen. The surgeries by Army doctors worked but would leave him with a slight limp and aching left knee throughout his life. He moved home with his mother, Louise, still living in Prentis Park. There were lots of war widows back then. A young beauty lived in the row house next door—Jennie Collier's daughter, a blond, hazel-eyed Georgia girl with a young son. Her name was Sarah, and her husband had vanished while flying an Air Force mission. Jennie and Louise were best friends and encouraged Alfred and Sarah to spend time together.

Sarah played along out of sympathy for the wounded veteran. She agreed to see Alfred because he seemed nice, he was lonely and lived one door away. Her brothers, sisters and her mother stoked the relationship. They loved young Alfred and quickly adopted him as a member of the Collier family. He had dinner with them, played cards with Sarah's brothers and spent nearly as much time in their home as his own.

Part of Sarah's reluctance was that she didn't like living in Portsmouth, wanting to return to Georgia or resettle in a less blue-collar town. Alfred, on the other hand, was a local guy and wanted to remain near family.

My father makes no pretense about his initial reaction to Sarah—he fell in love. She was witty, independent-minded and very bright. They complemented each other; she could be demanding and self-assured; he was amusing and doting, only wanting to make her happy.

Sarah might have appeared to be more aloof than Dad, but she was no less caring. She fell in love quickly with the modest, warm-hearted Alfred. They began to date.

Sarah accompanied Alfred on slow walks through the neighborhood. My dad took almost immediately to Sarah's child, David, whom he treated like his own son. He would pick up David and watch the boy when Sarah worked or ran errands. He took David for walks to a local park or for rides in his car. Sarah's brothers also helped care for the boy.

David is the half-brother who I never met. His life ended before I was born. It happened on a day Mother went downtown to buy school clothes for David. By this time, Alfred and Sarah were engaged to be married. Alfred had rented one of four bays in a garage directly across from the row house complex where he and mother were living. Their row homes didn't have garages, so the building on the opposite side of Elm Street was a convenient way for Dad to care for his car.

Dad and his best friend at the time were preparing to wash the car and had young David with them. Apparently, construction on the garage was incomplete because some live electrical wires had been dangling. David grabbed one of them. He was electrocuted. My father and his friend tried fiercely but in vain to save the boy. My father was nearly electrocuted himself while trying to pull David away from the live wire.

In the more than five decades they have been together, my mother has never blamed Alfred for the accident or even expressed anger toward him. My father, however, felt tremendous guilt and heartbreak, which eased over the decades, mostly because of my mother's magnanimity. However, Sarah's pain and her own self-flagellation over the loss of her first child never abated. She blamed herself for not being with David that day. She had gone in to town to buy him clothes for school. Had she only brought David with her or gone another time, she repeatedly thought over the many years.

Chapter IV
Life in the 'burbs

*"I never thought about being rich, but I realized at a
young age that money gave you independence."*

Sarah and Alfred had married in November 15, 1947,
holding a simple ceremony at church. My mother was ready
to start her new life and couldn't wait to be married again. She
looked beautiful on her wedding day and was surrounded by her
many brothers and sisters and my father's family. I was born
eleven months later, on October 10, 1948. Mother has often said
that I was the answer to her dreams. She wanted children again,
especially another son. She would wind up with me and Sharon,
who was born two and a half years after me.

I came real close to being named Stephen. An aunt just a
few months further along in her pregnancy beat my mom to
the punch and took the name Stephen for her son. I would be
named Daniel, or Danny, because of my mother's fondness for

Irish songs and names. My middle name is Alfred, after my dad.

Life was getting back on track for Alfred, who returned to the shipyard as a draftsman. He had enjoyed his work and those around him and was happy to be back. He had also reconnected with managers at the building supply store and resumed drawing blueprints in his spare time for homebuilders who purchased materials there.

Alfred wanted to build a house for his family but couldn't get a bank loan. You needed a big cash down payment back then, so he and Mother settled on a bungalow in Loxley Place, one of the many working class neighborhoods that sprouted to accommodate post-war shipyard families.

My parents stayed in Loxley a few years and enjoyed the camaraderie of the tightly packed streets lined with clapboard houses. However, Mother yearned for the quiet she had known as a country girl, and she wanted good, safe schools for her children. One of the men Dad worked for at the building supply store steered him toward a developer building a new community in Churchland, which was then mostly farms, creeks and bogs along the Western Branch of the Elizabeth River. When my parents first checked it out, there was nothing to the new community except a name: Sterling Point. But the developer promised that would soon change. Growth was coming to the suburbs. Get in early, Alfred was advised. The developer's forecast was dead-on; young families would come in droves.

The biggest carrot for my dad: The developer promised construction financing. For my mom, it was the quiet but not too isolated location; there were no other homes on this point of land yet, and it was surrounded by great water views. They sold their house in Loxley and rented another while their home was being built.

The lot they chose cost two thousand dollars. For another

five hundred they could have had waterfront. Mother said no thanks; she preferred the safety of being a couple of blocks away. She was afraid that her Danny or Sharon might wander out of sight and drown. David's death had made Mother zealously protective of me and my sister. We always felt loved, supported and safe, but Mother could also smother us with worry. Her love was a safety net and a cage.

Dad designed an eighteen-hundred-square-feet ranch-style house with three bedrooms, two bathrooms and a one-bay attached garage facing the street. The brick exterior upgrade added a thousand dollars to the price, bringing the total to fourteen thousand. We moved in 1954 when I was five and Sharon was two and a half. Our home was the first house on Bidgood Drive, named after the farm the community was built on.

As the developer promised, it didn't take long for other families to join us there. One was the Brunnels, whose son Rick was my age and would become one of my closest and most enduring friends. Most Sterling Point houses were modest but sturdy ranch homes like ours. Some of those on the water were much grander and built by well-off professionals. Growing up, I admired those homes.

There was an instant sense of community at Sterling Point. Young families had children who mingled freely around the protected enclave, running from yard to yard or through the woods buffering the community edges. There were no busy highways and plenty of parents stayed home during the day to keep a watchful eye. Most of us attended Churchland schools, which were expanding rapidly to accommodate the swell of students. In 1955, Churchland High School opened for grades nine through twelve.

I don't have many remarkable stories about my boyhood years because my childhood, neighborhood friends and family were pretty plain vanilla. I remember "The Adventures of Ozzie and Harriet," the ABC sitcom that aired from 1952 to 1966. It was like watching my life. My father was always calm, reasoned and buttoned-down, wearing a crisp-collared shirt and evenly knotted necktie. At home, he built model ships to relax, read the newspaper and rested in his favorite living room chair. His shoes were polished and his fair hair was combed away from his face and meticulously parted. In the mornings, Mom served bacon and eggs, grits or oatmeal. Dad sometimes ate with us and always left for work between seven-thirty and eight. Dinner was served each night, usually around four-thirty, the meal waiting for Dad when he came in the door. He was so punctual my mother often joked that she didn't think he had a real job.

Mother was attentive and immaculate. There were never dishes in the sink, unmade beds or clothes on the floor. Furniture was dusted and polished. Clothes were pressed, lunches were made. She always took an interest in my sister and me, asking about our day, our friends or our thoughts on some newsworthy subject.

Much of our social life and network of friends centered around church. Mother and Dad were raised Methodist but joined a Baptist congregation when we moved to Churchland. Sundays usually started with church service and then Sunday school. Sometimes we would attend a second service. There were lots of church picnics and dinners too. Dad would become a church deacon and I attended church-sponsored camps for at least two summers. Lots of our neighbors were part of the congregation, which made church activities less onerous because I had friends there too.

As a family, we joked and teased and sometimes lost patience with each other, but the tone was always civil. In church and in school, I would fidget. More than once, Mother had to sit in between my sister and me at church because of our clowning.

We could gauge Mother's anger by the intensity of her pinches. She'd clamp down if we were really acting up.

At home, she disciplined almost always with sharp stares or curt words. Mother rarely struck us, however, and when she did it was barely a tap. In fact, I don't ever remember a full-contact spanking. When we were younger and acted up, Mother would tell us to get a switch from the yard. I always picked the thinnest twig I could find. Mother would place the twig on top of the refrigerator and warn that if I acted up again, she would use it on my backside.

Dad was the proverbial Rock of Gibraltar, a nearly unflappable man who spoke softly and chose words carefully. There were really only two or three times that he lost his temper that I can recall: Once he rose from the dinner table, pushed his chair and walked off. I don't remember what brought that on, but it was an unusual and startling display. Another time, Dad removed his belt and snapped it when he saw that I had scribbled with crayons on a freshly painted wall. My mother heard the leather pop and dashed into the room. "Don't you dare hit him," she admonished. That brief episode is as close to an argument between the two that I can recall.

When it came to her kids, Mother was protective and unapologetic. If a neighbor or another adult criticized me, even unintentionally, my mother put up a quick defense. The mother of one of my best friends, who went on to become a commercial airline pilot, bragged about her son making all A's in school. Sarah retorted that she would rather see me make A's, B's and even C's and be well-rounded. Those expectations were fine with me.

My friends and I spent lots of time playing in the mud on the water's edge or fishing from the banks for bluegills or carp. We were all boy. We caught minnows and put them in jars, hunted for box turtles and ran from yard to yard playing cowboys. Mother would say that she never knew what I would pull from my pants pockets and remembers finding worms in them more than once.

I liked my friends, but I often liked being alone too. I still do. I found solitude a few blocks from home in a patch of woods that ended by the water. I especially liked sitting for hours by one large oak in particular, waiting quietly for fish to take the worms on a hook or dough balls made from bread that dangled from my line. If I caught a few panfish, Mom would cook them up.

I had lots of energy and preferred the outdoors over being confined to a wooden school desk. My first grade teacher thought I was too fidgety and complained to my mom. As usual, Mother defended her boy even though she pinched me for twitching while in church. At home and in private, however, she would make me sit still, more as practice than punishment.

Mom also knew I had a problem focusing on schoolwork. If I were a kid today, I might be diagnosed with Attention Deficit Disorder, although I'm certain my mother would not allow me to be tagged with such a label and certainly not speak of it to anyone. Mother enjoyed my vivaciousness and encouraged it. I dressed up in cowboy costumes or imitated someone I had seen on TV, like President John Kennedy. I liked to tell jokes and stories and enjoyed hearing them from others. I was a tease, especially with girls and women.

Sarah never let me far from her sight, especially in my youngest years. On my initial trips to my fishing spot down the street, she would secretly follow and stand behind trees and watch. She was most relaxed when I was home and preferred that my friends and I play in our yard, bribing us with treats. Dad outfitted the yard with swings and sliding boards to keep us entertained. I kept a worm bed next to the garage and critters in boxes and jars.

One of the scariest moments for my mother was when I fell from a neighbor's tree and broke my wrists. Mother was devastated, so much so that she needed almost as much consoling as me. My father didn't immediately rush me to the hospital because he wasn't certain how badly I was hurt. The swelling came on fast. As Dad took me to the ER, he was calm and reassuring. To this day, my mother, half-joking and half-serious, says that Alfred waited too long to take me to the hospital. Father just flashes a warm smile when she brings it up.

Dad was not one to shower me with embraces, even in the worst of times, such as the fall. "You just didn't put a lot of lovin' on a boy back then," Dad says. Sarah more than made up for that. She doted over me with hugs, patience, encouragement and protection. She was not a disciplinarian, but she wasn't a pushover, either. She drove me to Churchland Elementary School each morning and reviewed school assignments. On school days, she would call me into the house and make certain that I spent at least an hour in my room on homework and that my sister and I were in bed by eight-thirty.

Grandmother Jennie laid on the doting even thicker. She regularly stopped by the house, pretending to visit her daughter and son-in-law, but actually showered her attention on me. Granny had dozens of grandchildren, but I, at least according to my parents, sister and other family members, was her favorite. On holidays, I was the grandchild usually sitting in her lap. She would spin me in the air, lead me in a dance or sing to me in her thick Southern drawl. She'd listen to my stories and applauded if I did a little acting skit.

Granny always told me and my parents that I was special, that I would achieve a lot. She never predicted what path I might take, only that I would be a success. She injected me with confidence and a sense of security and helped me to believe in myself. Granny was also lots of fun. I remember driving with her in my Buick convertible, a cigar in my mouth and the two of us tossing soda cans at road signs. I would pick her up and carry her, or, when younger, grab her arms to dance. Grandma Jennie was my friend and much more. She loved me deeply, and I could feel that.

I have felt throughout my adult life that my grandmother has always guarded me in some metaphysical or spiritual way. There have been many inexplicable times when I spontaneously made some decision that proved fortunate or I escaped serious injury by inches or seconds. When I was eleven, a couple of friends and I headed over to get a closer look at a church being built just outside the neighborhood. I had seen plenty of buildings going up, but not one with a steeple and spire. Scaffolding stretched up the side of the building to the top and there were no workmen around, which was all the invitation I needed. Just as I reached the summit, I slipped, and in a flash I slid on my stomach down the domed slope and over the edge. Somehow, I grabbed one of the metal rails on the scaffolding, avoiding what surely would have been a devastating crash more than two stories below. I never told my grandmother that story or to this day, my mother, who would have locked me in my room until I was an adult.

Granny had a stroke later in life and needed to be placed in a nursing home. On my first visit I was overcome by the competing odors coming from incontinent patients and powerful disinfectants. I hated that my grandmother was in such a dreadful place. I promised her that I would one day have enough money to get her private care. I was thinking about that nursing home one afternoon when driving back to college. I had just driven past the North Carolina town where the nursing home was located. I stopped to get an ice cream, something Granny and I had often done together in Portsmouth. Minutes after I got back on the road, the inside of the car suddenly grew cool and damp. I felt Grandmother's spiritual presence in the seat next to me. It was eerie but comforting to know she was with me.

Granny's youngest brother, Larry, was unable to work throughout much of his life because of an illness. When I got older and had a little money, I sent Larry a check for two hundred and fifty dollars every month and continued to do so for twenty years until he died. I didn't know Larry that well and had no contact with him, but I sent him money because I thought it would have made my grandmother happy.

It's clear to me now when I look back on my early years that Mom and Granny enhanced my self-esteem by emphasizing what I could achieve, not what was out of reach or lacking. They were my emotional safety net. If I brought home a bad report card or test, Mother would say that I could do better, but she wouldn't scold me. Granny would shrug it off. They encouraged me to try harder and reassured me that I was capable if I applied myself. They made excuses for me.

My dad once mentioned to Mom that I wasn't hitting the ball well on my little league team. In fact, I had only had a few hits all season. Mother indignantly proclaimed that it was Father's fault for making me nervous. When I got into trouble for throwing darts into the back of my bedroom door instead of the dartboard, mother again defended me, saying it was better than playing darts somewhere else and getting hurt.

Looking back, I see now that my parents simply wanted me to be a balanced and happy person who was considerate of others, who had friends, who enjoyed life. In school I made a B or better in subjects I enjoyed, such as history, and scored less so in other areas; but I feel like I received an A in self-esteem, which I believe propelled me further in life than acing geography or algebra might have.

I was a curious kid who asked lots of questions at dinner and of guests. I liked to quiz others about themselves, another trait that would serve me well in business. Adults and kids would tell me stories or secrets. I reinforced the positives, rather than judge them, just as my parents did with me. I quickly learned that most everyone wants to feel good about themselves by sharing their successes and to focus on what we have in common, not what sets us apart.

Neither of my parents were strident idealists. We were churchgoers but not zealously religious or political. Sarah often leaned more toward Republican candidates, despite her reverence for the great FDR. Dad voted for the person, not the party. He was an Independent long before it became fashionable. There were no placards on our lawn or political bumper stickers on our cars. I have followed my dad's lead when it comes to politics and politicians. The individual is more important than the political party. There are honorable and trustworthy members of each political persuasion just as there are arrogant liars. "Vote for the man," my father often said.

We lived modestly but I never felt our family needed more. Sure, I admired the big houses and fancy cars in others' driveways, but that didn't make me feel envious or inadequate. My sister and I received nice presents on birthdays and Christmas. Mom would make sure we were smartly dressed and that we each had a quarter in our pockets when out visiting.

I liked having my own money, even as a boy. It made feel independent and spared me from asking for handouts from Mom and Dad. I was that familiar kid who in the spring and summer cut neighbors' lawns using my dad's gas and lawnmower. I had about five clients who paid me two dollars per mow. I once loaned a friend a few dollars, fully expecting to be repaid. My mother told me that if I could afford to loan the money to my friend, I could afford to give it to him. I didn't like the sound of that and would later in life figure out what she really meant.

Friends and relatives say I was a generous kid with an easy smile who was quick to laugh. I blame that on my Uncle Carl Argo. Most people are fortunate to have one great set of parents and siblings. I had hit the lottery and had two sets: Sarah and Alfred, of course, and Uncle Carl and my mother's sister Helen. Uncle Carl and Aunt Helen treated me like a son, and their daughter, Linda, was like having another sister. As a young boy, the Argos would take me with them for weekends at Nags Head. Back then, there was a two-lane road that ran along the beach and only a few small motels and a couple of restaurants.

Uncle Carl loved to fish and be around water. But he didn't like being in it or on it in a boat. He had almost drowned as a boy and wasn't about to tempt fate again. He was a stout man, a fireplug who played football as a kid, someone who looked like he could bash through a brick wall with his shoulders. His temperament, however, was more lamb than lion. He was approachable, friendly and self-effacing.

Back home, he would often take me to the Lynnhaven Pier in Virginia Beach or to spin for largemouth bass on a local lake. At Nags Head, we'd either cast from the beach or a fishing pier. Aunt Helen was content to sit in the sand and read. Going out on the pier made her feel seasick, she said. As an adult, I sustained the tradition of taking Nags Head fishing trips with Uncle Carl. I would drive him to the beach for a weekend or we would stay at my vacation house on the Outer Banks. I even coaxed Uncle Carl onto one of my boats and took him fishing offshore.

I never forgot how Uncle Carl indulged my endless questions

and did his best to answer them. He was also a jokester, another trait he encouraged in me. We once went to visit a friend of his who lived like a slob. A greasy car engine sat in the middle of the guy's living room and there were grime and oil stains everywhere, including on his hands. The guy asked Uncle Carl if he would like a snack. Uncle Carl politely declined and then said, "Nothing for me, thanks, but I think Danny would like a sandwich. Would you make him one?"

Uncle Carl was as much of a friend as a surrogate parent. I could confide in him and would for years to come. He was a humble guy who came from the same rural area in Georgia as my mother. His first job in Portsmouth was delivering milk with a horse and buggy. He used to say that the horse did all of the work, including remembering the delivery route. Later, he served in World War II and afterward was a systems flight engineer with the Navy.

Uncle Carl was another calming and cheerful influence, a common guy with a forgiving heart. On a fishing trip, I had cast one of my fishing rods, which slipped from my hands, flew into the Bay and sunk to the bottom. I was embarrassed and felt awful about losing the rod and reel. Uncle Carl just laughed. He and Aunt Helen also bought me my first car, an old Ford that had been repossessed by a local bank. Even as a teenager, I continued my frequent visits to hang out with Uncle Carl or have dinner at his house. He was my buddy, someone I could trust completely. Shortly after I earned my driver's license, I bragged to Uncle Carl about how fast I and some friends had been driving. He was worried I might get hurt, so much so he said something to Aunt Helen. The next time I saw them, she pulled me aside and gave me a soft but no-nonsense warning to be careful. "Danny, I really don't want to have to say anything to your mom and dad, but you need to be careful with your driving. You could be seriously hurt, and you know what that would do to your mother."

Neither she nor Uncle Carl ever said anything to my parents. No doubt that Aunt Helen knew my mom would about lose her mind at the thought of me speeding around on back roads with friends. If she continued to let me drive at all, Sarah would have sat in the back seat supervising every trip. I took Aunt Helen's admonishment to heart.

The Argos often joined Dad, Mom, Sharon and me on several of our summer vacations. We almost always brought some family member with us on these annual trips. Mother saved for them all year. Each week, she would take five or ten dollars and slip it into her Bible, building a nice stash for our sojourn.

Most of the trips were unstructured. The adults would decide on a destination in advance and then, without much of a travel plan, we would load into my dad's car and hit the road. I remember his packed Studebaker well. Movies have been made about the absurdity or horror of family vacations. Ours were generally pleasant, even without an itinerary.

We mostly traveled the Eastern Seaboard, visiting family in Georgia or heading to the mountains of western Virginia. We even camped in tents that collapsed on us. Dad would drive until dark, and then we would look for a suitable motel or lodge. Mother would inspect the rooms. More than once she declared a place too expensive or dirty. Mother often had the final word.

My dad remained consistently calm and patient as he chauffeured us around on those meandering journeys. He was also remarkably unflappable as my baseball coach. I wasn't very good when I first started playing the game. I struck out a lot and made some errors playing first base. No matter how poorly I performed, Dad encouraged me. He would say I would do better next time or that "everyone has an off day" or that "we'll work on a few fundamentals." He never showed disappointment when we lost, not to me or others on the team. If we won, he didn't gloat or prance, either. In time, I did get better at the game. As I grew, my coordination improved and I could hit the ball a long way. I thank Dad for that.

People liked my dad and sometimes, without explanation, would show him and me great kindness or generosity. Our dentist, Dr. Parker, had a small office without a receptionist. I remember he charged three dollars and seventy five cents to fill a cavity without Novocain. He took care of our teeth for free—*with* Novocain. There was a local policeman who would take me for rides in his squad car and on visits to the station. Then there were the guys at a local auto repair shop who let me hang around and watch them work and joke. These were good, hard-working Portsmouth people who watched out for neighbors and friends. These were good times in a "Mayberry R.F.D."-like world.

My dad and I spent most Saturday mornings together. We would go to the butcher shop or get a haircut or go fishing. It was on one of those Saturdays that he took me to the shipyard for "the visit." Perhaps I had been too sheltered, but I had never seen anyone act as rude or cruel as that security guard at the shipyard entrance gate. He was demeaning, dismissing my father as if he were a vagrant. He scolded my dad, telling him kids were not allowed in the yard and that he should know better. He wasn't going to allow him in; the guard didn't care who my dad was or where he worked.

Dad remained humble, not wanting to be further embarrassed or to cause a commotion. He spoke reverently and quietly to the guard, who eventually allowed us to pass and enter my dad's office building. My anger rose as we toured his workplace. No one should be so disrespected, I thought, especially not a gentle soul like Alfred Hoffler. I didn't know what occupation I might pursue, but I knew at that moment that I wanted to be in control of my own destiny, that I wanted someday to be my own boss.

I didn't know in high school or even immediately afterward what I wanted to do for a living. High school, like my early years, was a fun, largely trouble-free time. I sprouted to more than six feet and wrestled in the one-hundred-and-forty-pound weight class. Like so many guys my age, I was into cars, going to the drive-in, hanging out. We were clean-cut and preppy.

Most in my crowd kept their car or transistor radios tuned to competing radio stations WGH or WNOR. Each week they would list the top thirty songs. The Beatles, Elvis and Motown were hugely popular with us and were the music of choice at our age eighteen-and-under dances at the Churchland American Legion Hall. Admission was a quarter, making for a cheap date.

Churchland High was a long way from the hippie and drug culture of the mid-1960s. One assistant principal would stop boys with Beatles haircuts to make certain their bangs were suitably above their eyebrows. There was no tie-dye or T-shirts, either. Most of the guys dressed in argyle sweaters and khaki pants or short sleeves with collars.

We drank beer, an occasional bottle of cheap wine, or if someone was daring, they would spike the fruit punch at a dance or party with grain alcohol. We did stupid stuff and acted our age. But we stayed away from pot and other drugs. There were only about two hundred and fifty in my graduating class, so most of us knew each other as did many of our parents. It was easier in some ways to keep track of what kids were up to then, mostly because all of us pretty much did the same stuff and hung out in the same places. Churchland was a village within a town.

My growing independence as a teen became tough on my mom. When I was out at night, she would sit in the den and rock nervously until I was home safe. Dad was often snoozing, something that perplexed my mother. How could he sleep? I kept my escapades largely a secret to avoid worrying her further, giving her only sanitized versions. The bad stuff was pretty mild by today's standards. I never got in trouble with the police and I never got in a fight—never. I learned pretty early that most people wind up in a worse place when they use their fists. Fighting brings you down and can be distracting. Even as a kid, I gravitated toward people who were upbeat and fun to be around and certainly not violent.

My Uncle Bill was like that. He was a jovial guy, full of smiles and laughs. One of his friends opened a tavern in 1966 that became a community hangout as much as a watering hole. Uncle Bill introduced me to Edward B. Speers, owner and operator of the restaurant bearing his name. Eddie was a Churchland-born community gadfly who made friends quickly and liked to talk about local and world events.

Like my dad, Eddie was a product of his generation, a WWII hero who spent twenty-four years in the Navy. Eddie served on a ship sunk by a torpedo while patrolling near Guadalcanal. And he was one of nine men who risked their lives by swimming in the darkness and heavy swells to rescue survivors of two Navy ships, the USS Langley and USS Pecos.

Each Sunday morning, Eddie's tavern filled with regulars, including my uncle, who came in for coffee, breakfast and discussion. Some came to escape church, including me. When I became old enough to drive, I would pretend I was heading to church but instead, head to Eddie's. On one of my first trips there, I was so excited that I left my car in neutral and didn't put on the emergency brake. Just as I was about to enter the tavern, I noticed my car rolling down a slight hill, heading for a tree. Luckily it missed the tree and other cars. That was yet another story I never told my mom.

Hanging out with Eddie and some of the regulars piqued my interest in civic affairs and provided me with a fly-on-the-wall view of how grassroots politics works. Several in Eddie's clique served on local boards, commissions or council. Eddie himself was active politically, and in 1974 he was elected to his first of two terms as a Chesapeake councilman. My friendship with Eddie would give me a leg up later in life after I started my company. He was on the council from 1980 to 1984, the years we launched Armada Hoffler. Of course, back when I was in high school, I had no way of knowing how this relationship with Eddie would carry forward. As a teenager, and later as a college student, I visited Eddie simply because I liked him and he showed an interest in me.

One aspect of my personal life that eased my mother's worry during my teen years was my high school sweetheart, Mary Jo Wetmore. She lived in a nearby neighborhood and attended Catholic school. She was a shy, sweet girl with long dark hair and a big smile. Like my parents, Mary Jo's were involved with their church.

Mary Jo and I met on a blind date. After a movie, we went to a nearby Shoney's. While at our booth, I pulled a picture from my wallet of a hideous-looking middle-age woman. I told Mary Jo the picture was of my mother and that I wanted to prepare her before I brought her home later that night to meet my parents—that my mother was sensitive about her looks and that she didn't like it when people stared at her. We all got a good laugh when Mary Jo met my mom, who of course looked nothing like the deformed woman in the photograph. My parents liked her immediately and warned her about my teasing.

The buttoned-down culture at Mary Jo's Catholic school mirrored that of Churchland High, so she had no trouble fitting in with my crowd. If anything, the Catholic kids were more liberal than a lot of my more Protestant preppy friends. Mary Jo wore her long hair pulled back. Her mom was an executive in a company that built tennis courts. Businesswomen with rank were a rarity in those pre-Woodstock days.

Mary Jo's mom allowed her to transfer to Churchland in her junior year, mostly to take courses not available at the Catholic high school and also to be with me. Mary Jo, unlike me, was a serious student who knew from a young age exactly what she wanted to be—a schoolteacher.

Mary Jo and I planned to be together but agreed that college would come first. In fact, she made it clear that she wouldn't marry me until we graduated. There was a second compelling reason that I needed to go to college. The Vietnam War was raging and the draft was in full force. My grades were unimpressive, except in a few courses that I liked, including history and current events. My parents were patriotic and loved their country, but Mother had lost her first husband and a brother in one war, and my dad nearly lost his life. Serving in Vietnam was simply out of the question for me, my mother insisted.

As graduation neared, a school guidance counselor called my parents at home to set up a meeting at school with the three of us. When we met, the counselor was blunt. She said I wasn't college material and that my parents should put the money they would have spent on my college tuition in a savings account for me instead. I would need it, because the best I could hope for, the counselor said, was to eke out a living as a tradesman. She recommended that I become a brick mason. Mother fired back with indignation, "I will decide if my son goes to college."

Chapter V
Getting Started

"Success is a gradual thing. You fall into it.
It becomes part of your life."

Mother enrolled me in a community college in North Carolina. The time had come for me to get more serious about my studies. Mary Jo still had a year of high school, so I'd often go home on weekends to visit her, which of course meant that I stayed with my parents. There wasn't much of a social life at my college, and I was anxious to move on. For my final two years, I transferred to Campbell College, now Campbell University, to earn a bachelor's degree in business studies. The campus, located thirty miles south of Raleigh, was about a four-hour drive from Portsmouth and two hours from Mary Jo, who had enrolled at Averett University in Danville, Virginia.

At Campbell, I noticed almost immediately that a lot of the other students living in the dorms got hungry at night after the cafeteria closed. Except for vending machines, there weren't many choices for snacks. Suddenly, something I learned in class made sense—supply and demand.

I kept a sandwich maker in my dorm room, the kind that presses together to heat bread evenly from both sides. Word quickly spread that I made grilled cheese sandwiches on demand. This proved to a very profitable venture with a steep growth curve. As the dollars poured in, my menu expanded to include different choices of grilled cheese, some soft drinks and bags of pretzels and potato chips. Demand surged during exam weeks, when students were up late cramming. I made about one hundred dollars a week, more than enough to cover my expenses. My pockets were often stuffed with ones and fives. At times, I felt like a bookie. I knew then that majoring in business was the right choice. I also knew what aspects of business weren't for me.

Accounting, statistics and the various "numbers" courses required in business school were a killer combination of boring and strenuous. I recognized the importance of reading spreadsheets and figuring percentages, but doing that work felt lifeless and impersonal. Marketing and sales, on the other hand, got me excited. It was the frontline of the competitive world. It involved understanding people as well as products and then marrying the two. It was making money, not just counting it.

With my bachelor's degree under arm, I headed back to Portsmouth in the spring of 1971. Jobs weren't easy to come by. The Vietnam War was winding down and the national economy sputtered just as the first big wave of baby boomers looked for work. The unemployment rate that year hovered near nine percent in some cities. The country remained divided and embittered about Vietnam. The greatest fighter of all time, "conscientious objector" Muhammad Ali, was pummeled that year by Smokin' Joe Frazier in Madison Square Garden. Pop,

Motown and rock also vied for young hearts and minds with words of joy, hope or despair. The Osmonds released "One Bad Apple," Three Dog Night topped the charts with "Joy to the World," and Marvin Gaye asked "What's Going On." The country's conflicted mood and its politics intrigued me, but all I really wanted was a job.

Not long after I graduated, Mary Jo and I were shopping at a Portsmouth grocery store when we bumped into my childhood and high school buddy Rick Burnell. I tried not to seem too down in front of my friend, but employment was proving elusive. Rick had just graduated from Old Dominion University in Norfolk, Virginia, and landed a position with a local branch office of Dun & Bradstreet. I felt happy for him but even worse for myself.

Rick had worked on school newspapers and was skillful at research and writing. Like me, he was also interested in business. Rick was smart, well-spoken, clean-cut and upbeat. D&B smartly hired him to research and write reports on the financial health of companies. Banks or supply chains purchased the reports to help determine the worthiness of a company seeking a loan, building materials or a line of credit. Those applying had to oblige D&B by opening their books to credit researchers like Rick.

These, of course, were the pre-email, pre-Google days when doing financial research meant flipping through paper records and financial ledgers stored in boxes and making phone calls during regular business hours. There were often tight deadlines for when the reports were due, which meant working fast and often typing into the evening.

Credit reporting agencies were notorious in their early years for making sweeping characterizations about individuals, conclusions that went beyond cash flow and tax returns. Rick remembers finding an old report from the 1950s shoved in the back of a filing cabinet. It alleged that a Hampton Roads businessman with an Italian last name may have had financial ties to La Cosa Nostra. The guy was in the construction business and trying to get bank financing for a project. No one knew for sure where or how the man got started in business, so it was assumed by the report writer that the guy had to be mob connected. Those printed rumors were never substantiated and that person went on to become a great success as a legitimate businessman. Thankfully, few beyond Rick ever saw that report.

Rick said he was enjoying his new job and told me there was an opening in in his department at the D&B office in Norfolk. Rick got me an interview, and I got the job. Writing reports wasn't my forte or passion, especially not the boilerplate, stick-to-the-numbers iterations. But being a report writer and researcher was an opportunity to become part of a significant and well-respected firm. It was a foot in the door. With persistence and a sprinkle of luck, I might get transferred into sales.

D&B, along with branches of other big-name companies, like Xerox and Honeywell, were clustered in the Kroger industrial park just outside of downtown Norfolk. Part of the business trend back then was to leave old urban centers for the suburbs, which offered large parking lots and plenty of office space to expand.

The D&B office was on the first floor and sparingly appointed. We had a teletype machine and an offset press to print our reports. We typed them up, checked them for grammar and spelling and then set them for the press. If the customer wanted two sets, we rolled two off the press. If other businesses wanted the same report, we'd print another. It was a pay-on-demand setup, which sometimes meant hand delivering reports to anxious clients.

Our workstations were blandly outfitted with telephones

and typewriters. The pay wasn't all that attractive, either. Mary Jo would earn eighteen thousand a year teaching school for nine months, a thousand more than my salary at D&B. I kept reminding myself that I was just getting started.

Almost from my first week, I began angling for a job in sales. I remember how impressed I was with Joe McDonald, the office's first-string salesman and manager. Joe would grab a bell sitting on the receptionist's desk and ring it every time he made a sale. The rest of us would cheer from our desks because that ring meant revenue—and job security.

Joe's job was to find new customers for reports we had on file or to persuade banks and others to use D&B services when they needed information on prospective or existing customers. That meant lots of hand shaking, business lunches and prospecting, all of which appealed to me. I couldn't wait to be liberated from my typewriter and desk and launch into the real world. My desk job at D&B was like being in a high school classroom again.

My break came after about eight months, when one of Joe's assistants left. By then, Joe knew me well. I tactfully adopted him as a mentor and showed him great admiration, which was genuine. I was a baby-faced kid with shaggy hair from a small college and protective home, but Joe liked me and figured that if this lad could sell himself to a salesman, he should do pretty well endearing himself to others.

Joe and other D&B salesmen had tilled the Hampton Roads business turf long and hard, so I decided to strike out into virgin territory, heading south to the Outer Banks and a few other North Carolina communities along the way. I had some ideas about where I might cast my line, but nothing hard-and-fast. I just did what salesmen do—I knocked on doors. The Outer Banks wasn't that different from any other community, it was just smaller. It had furniture stores, a few lumber yards and building-supply centers, a couple of local banks, hotels and several small incorporated towns. Local governments spend lots of money on services, and they also like recruiting businesses to their communities. Our credit reports might prove useful.

It was a magical few days. Nearly every business I visited had never been approached by D&B or any other credit reporting agency. It was also true that the communities along the Outer Banks, places like Nags Head and Kitty Hawk, were growing at a pretty fast clip. Wider roads and bridges made OBX more accessible, opening the floodgates for development.

My junket proved fortuitous. In a good month, a D&B salesman might sell four or five contracts. I sold that many in a week. I also scored some sales in growing Virginia Beach. I was ringing that bell at the receptionist's desk a lot.

Each year, D&B's national office in New York hosted a banquet for its top sales associates. I had only been selling for about a year but received an invite. I was married then, and Mary Jo and I were living comfortably but on a tight budget. A trip to New York on the company dime would be a treat.

There were six or so people at each table. I didn't know any of the others sitting at mine. There was lots of excitement, chatter and drinks. One of the men at my table was older than the rest of us and better dressed. He seemed relaxed and personable, shaking hands and trading smiles with others who stopped by to greet him. I could see why others liked him.

He was very curious about me and my background. He wanted to know about where I was raised, my parents, siblings, hobbies, ambitions. He asked Mary Jo about her job and about where we lived. He then apologized for not properly introducing himself. I had never heard of the guy before. "You really don't know who I am, do you?" he asked. I said I was sorry and confessed my ignorance. "It's no mistake that I am sitting at your table," he said.

The man informed us that he was a top executive from D&B's corporate office. He wanted to know how I had sold five contracts in just a few days. It had never been done before, anywhere, by a D&B salesman. He then asked me an array of questions about the Hampton Roads market and my approach to selling. That dinner felt more like a job interview than a celebration. When I returned to Norfolk, I knew why. I had been promoted to head marketing and sales in the Norfolk office. The timing was good, because my friend Joe McDonald had announced his retirement.

More than thirty people were now under my direction. Some were happy for me and others resentful that they would be reporting to a kid in his twenties who had been there less than two years. I didn't let that bother me and reciprocated by treating everyone with respect. I would work closest with those who were receptive to me and most enthusiastic about our work. This promotion became a crash course in managing people, which has more to do with understanding human psychology than accounting principles.

I spent nearly four years in that office, becoming more confident each month. Working for D&B exposed me to lots of business people, some of the region's most influential. It also made me realize the power of networking. It became apparent that personal and business relationships often merged. People seemed more inclined to do business with people they were personally comfortable with.

One of the simplest ways to impress others is the most basic: Remember their names. Mary Jo helped me with that in the early years of my career. After a dinner or party, Mary Jo would write the names of people we had met in a notebook. She would note their kids' names too. If those kids were in college, she would also jot that down.

Mary Jo or I would try to find out in advance the names of those attending dinners or parties we were going to. On our drives there, we would go over the list to refresh our memories; the name of the wife of so-and-so is; their daughter is a junior at so-and-so university.

Networking led me to Walter Alford, the head of economic development for Virginia Beach. He was a key client of D&B and very plugged in politically. Much of his job was prospecting for businesses looking to relocate or expand. Economic development directors are, and continue to be, dealmakers. They use tax incentives or desirable plots of land to lure businesses that, in return, create jobs for local folks who then buy houses and feed city coffers by paying taxes.

Courting business prospects can be expensive and time consuming. D&B financial reports helped to make that job easier. Guys like Walter used them to distinguish between strong companies with plans to expand and companies struggling to remain afloat. They can help business recruiters determine who can back up expansion plans with financing and who can't keep the lights on.

Walter and I spent lots of time over drinks and dinner discussing business and, of course, personal stuff. He was an affable guy with a lot of contacts and a vision of how the region would grow. He could sense the building demand for industrial and warehouse space and knew that lots of cities had industrial parks and airports with special tax breaks.

Walter decided to jump from public service into the development world, signing on as a vice president with the development company Eastern International. Not long after, he asked me to join him as sales and marketing chief. My stay with

Eastern International was brief but fruitful. Although based in Virginia Beach, the company had dealings with investors and others in New York and elsewhere. My network of associates and friends expanded exponentially. Part of my job was to find businesses that might want to buy space in one of our buildings, develop land we owned or find investment partners.

Walter taught me more than any college could about making land deals and consummating them. Basically, the business climate is like the weather. You have to act while the sun is shining. Walter taught me never to dawdle. If you have someone who is ready to do a deal, act quickly. Walter was dead-on right. I have seen more than one deal evaporate because of delays and vacillating.

My experience with Eastern International cemented my interest in land development. It felt like a perfect nexus of finance and sales. I learned how deals were fashioned. I had lots of connections, and like Walter, I could see where business in Hampton Roads was heading.

Chapter VI
Armada

*"People become interested in you when you
become interested in them."*

I was spending more and more time in New York for business and for fun. I had met several people at the start of their careers with as much ambition as me. It was already apparent that who you know is worth at least as much as what you know— maybe even more in my line of work. A friend led me to Dun & Bradstreet, which led me to Eastern International. As my world expanded, my ideas for career and success evolved too. The seeds of confidence so meticulously planted in me by my parents and grandmother had taken root. I wanted something bigger than a job; I wanted an opportunity to be self-made and self-directed. I didn't have to look much beyond my hometown to find those things.

The push to the suburbs that landed my family in Churchland

continued its surge throughout Hampton Roads. Populations in the region's older core were declining. Growth was pushing south into Chesapeake, which had largely been farmland when I was growing up and even in the late 1970s was still viewed as the hinterlands of Hampton Roads. Virginia Beach was a different story. It was no longer just a resort strip with hoity homes on the north end and a few hotels and bungalows in the rental district. The region's plethora of Navy and Marine bases supplied the area with a skilled labor pool, young families and lots of retirees. The residents needed homes and businesses needed offices, stores and warehouses.

Norfolk was still very much the power and cultural center of the region. Banks, commercial real estate and law firms congregated there. Many of the mover and shakers were from "old money" or had married into it. It was a cliquish group that played tennis together, attended the same Protestant churches, barbequed at the yacht club and hosted weddings at the Botanical Gardens. This circle of bankers, lawyers, railroad executives and landowners collaborated on deals and often brought new business to town. They also significantly influenced who held elected office, and they could ostracize those who worked against them. By and large, these were honorable men with good intentions. But as with so many towns, Norfolk's ruling class practiced a passive elitism that even today ruffles businessmen and leaders from neighboring cities.

Being from Portsmouth definitely placed me outside of Norfolk's inner circle. Portsmouth was the blue-collar town across the Elizabeth River. The two cities were within eyesight of each other, connected by bridge tunnels and passenger ferry boats. They shared much the same rich history, being formed during the colonialist days, building ships for the Navy and battling the North during the Civil War. Yet Portsmouth and Norfolk behaved like sibling rivals, rarely cooperating and often acting snobbish or jealous toward each other.

Instead of trying to work through Norfolk's establishment, I decided to go around it. Chesapeake, which borders Portsmouth to the west and south, was quietly, but persistently, growing. Its population had long surpassed the one hundred thousand or so living in Portsmouth. Chesapeake was also quickly gaining on Norfolk, which would soon dip below two hundred thousand residents. Residents and businesses wanted to be in the suburbs, and Chesapeake had the space to accommodate that sprawl.

Unlike Norfolk, Portsmouth and even Virginia Beach, Chesapeake lacked a distinguishable center. Its courts and city hall were down in the Great Bridge area, which was slighted as little more than a northern outpost of North Carolina. It was a village surrounded by farmers and only about ten miles from the Carolina border. But there was this other section of the city, closer to Virginia Beach and Norfolk's epicenter.

The region's main highway, Interstate 64, ran through the middle of Greenbrier, named after a Chesapeake tree nursery that grew acres of shrubs and trees. As a teenager, I hunted quail on the flat, somewhat swampy fields there. It was just a few miles from where I-64 intersected with I-264, the other major highway that ran through the region, connecting Portsmouth and Norfolk to Virginia Beach and the Oceanfront.

There was another not so subtle shift descending on Hampton Roads that would goose the region's population shifts: Defense spending was poised to ramp up. President Nixon had cut the defense budget by almost thirty percent after ending the Vietnam War. The trend continued throughout most of the 1970s. Generals, admirals and some hawkish politicians, including a former California governor running for president, argued that the cuts went too deep and that the country was vulnerable to the Soviets. It was time to restore our military might, which meant that area shipyards would soon be busy again and the Navy would be hiring sailors, a double shot of adrenaline for Hampton Roads. If logic followed, that also meant that companies that supply the Navy, Marines and other armed services with everything from toilet seats to radar screens would want to set up shop locally and need space to store parts. There were two locations that, in my view, would be perfect for the supply warehouses and office buildings they would need. One was a hotel site off Diamond Springs Road in the heart of Virginia Beach. It was a dump, literally a whorehouse on nine acres, located conveniently close to several Navy bases. The other tract was one hundred acres of woods and fields in Chesapeake, abutting Greenbrier Parkway and I-64.

An investment company called Greenbrier Associates recognized the potential of the area and had purchased much of the old tree nursery and some surrounding land. The owners were from out of state and had dispatched lawyers and engineers to have the land subdivided and approved for development. Greenbrier worked with local contractors, building housing and retail space. But the company was also in the business of reselling land to raise some cash.

I saw no point in competing with Greenbrier or others that were feeding the housing boom. Instead, I wanted to be the go-to guy for businesses in need of offices and warehouses. A new concept for commercial space had started to emerge in some larger cities around the country, generically referred to as "flex" space. The idea was to supply buildings that would double as an office and warehouse. Until that time, businesses would often have to buy or lease separate buildings in different locations—a warehouse in an industrial park and offices in a downtown or pedestrian area. With flex space, a company would only need a single building. A plumbing supply store, for example, could carve out a small office and counter in the front of a building and use the rest of the space to store inventory. One of the problems I saw was that warehouses were often ugly buildings tucked away in old industrial parks or inaccessible locations. These warehouses were sometimes gritty and next to even less attractive heavy industry or assembly plants.

Warehouse and office space could be compatible and made to look attractive. The concept was pretty simple: Design the front of buildings with the same curb appeal as full-fledged offices and design loading platforms and huge bay doors in the back and out of view. Providing stylish exteriors would mesh well with other commercial buildings that might wish to locate nearby, such as hotels and other professional offices.

I approached Greenbrier Associates, which said it would sell the land off the Interstate for twenty thousand dollars an acre. Greenbrier had built a huge retention pond on the site for drainage, and the land had the necessary zoning for commercial buildings. Of the one hundred acres, about seventy could be developed. While in discussions with Greenbrier, I also negotiated a purchase price of three hundred and twelve thousand dollars for the old hotel off Diamond Springs Road. Through my contacts in Virginia Beach, I had heard that a company already located off Diamond Springs wanted to expand and needed two or three additional warehouses. I also formed a list of other prospects for the Greenbrier site, mostly defense-related high-tech companies.

Now, I needed money.

Among the many people I met in New York when I was with Dun & Bradstreet and Eastern International was Peter Nitze and Frank Stagen, owners of a financial consulting business. Nitze-Stagen had a client with a lot of money to invest, a Texas oilman looking to diversify into real estate. The company, Armada Petroleum, had made hundreds of millions of dollars in just about every aspect of the oil business. The Houston-based Armada had offices in Geneva, New York and London, and business associates around the world, including Saudi Arabia.

The oil business surges through boom-and-bust cycles and in the mid-1970s, it had been roaring. In the fall of 1973, the Arab nations of OPEC, the Organization of Petroleum Exporting Countries, slapped the U.S. with an embargo because we supported Israel in the Yom Kippur War. With supplies choked off, American drivers were forced to wait in long lines to gas up. The energy crisis was so bad that the lights on the national Christmas tree weren't turned on that December to save energy. The U.S. economy got walloped with stock prices plunging forty percent. Our economy and sense of security were in a tailspin because of a perceived energy shortage.

Wildcatters from Texas and the Southwest responded in force. Improved drilling methods and geologic science unleashed an army of independent riggers and explorers backed by oil entrepreneurs anxious to discover, buy and refine domestic crude. These spirited risk takers drilled nine times as many wells in the 1970s as the huge international conglomerates. The conglomerates provided seed money and men in the field anted up grit and determination. It was supply and demand at its rawest and most daring.

Armada Petroleum was one of the many independents to join the stampede. It was headed by a debonair businessman with a degree in chemical engineering from Texas A&M, James E. Fisher. Jim had been in the oil business since the early 1960s and made a fortune buying and shipping Texas crude around the world and financing domestic explorations. He was at the epicenter of a boom that, a decade earlier, created a wave of more than seven hundred mergers and acquisitions of oil explores, traders and refiners. Jim worked for some of the smallest and biggest. His résumé included stints with Sinclair

Oil and Atlantic Richfield Company, better known as ARCO. Jim eventually struck out on his own as a consultant and, riding the oil-boom momentum, formed Armada Petroleum in 1974. He was, as he put it, one of the small guys trying to move fast and feed the burgeoning demand from a country shocked by how dependent it had become on oil imports.

Jim often did business with a handshake or telephone call. He was well-known throughout the industry as a savvy risk taker who kept his word. With backing from the big players and a promise from them to buy, Jim became an explorer, buyer and seller of crude. In just four years, he had built Armada Petroleum into a two-billion-dollar business.

By 1978, the tide of the fickle oil industry shifted again. The federal government had imposed a tight regulatory grip on crude pricing as a result of OPEC giving a lot of oil traders fits. By the end of the decade, regulators were enforcing a series of complex laws aimed at leveling crude prices. Those refining "old oil" from domestic wells had to, in effect, subsidize refiners importing more expensive "new oil." This system was intended to keep as many refiners in business as possible, which in theory would increase oil supplies and stabilize gas prices. But for some free marketers, it was government meddling at its worst.

Armada Petroleum decided to shift some of its wealth into land development as a hedge. Fisher and his partners could see that money was being made by building and leasing commercial offices. The company owned land and invested in a few small office building projects in New York, Philadelphia, Houston and Dallas. Fisher didn't know much about land development, but he did know that fully leased office buildings could throw off lots of cash, so Jim decided to take calculated risks, just as he had in the free-wielding days of wildcatting for crude in the Southwest desert. The word circulated in New York and elsewhere that Armada Petroleum had money to spend and was looking for a partner.

Jim was intrigued by the stories he was told about this young guy from Virginia with some big ambitions. His partners did some checking around about Hampton Roads and about me and in October 1979, about a week before my thirty-first birthday, a meeting was set. I was advised to stay in the Whitehall Hotel, now the Crowne Plaza, which was next to Armada Petroleum's downtown Houston headquarters. Mr. Fisher, I was told, was a man of class and substance. He was known as a gentleman and impeccable dresser. I didn't want to come off as something less, so I got a haircut, packed my best suit and booked a room at the swanky hotel.

I didn't think I heard the reservations clerk right when she quoted me two hundred and ten dollars for one night. That was almost a monthly mortgage payment on my home. I was doing better financially at the time, earning about thirty-five thousand in salary with Eastern International. But still, my budget was tight.

Mary Jo and I had our first child, Sara, about a year earlier, naming her after my mom, but without the letter "h" in her name. We had just moved from a townhouse in an old but historic section of Portsmouth into a modest three-bedroom home in a suburban community just west of where I was raised. Mary Jo supported my desire to launch my own company and had tolerated, but not fully embraced, the many business dinners and parties that brought us to this point.

Mary Jo enjoyed our family time together and was happiest when we drove on summer weekends to Nags Head on North Carolina's Outer Banks with her mother and our daughter. I would fish in the surf while they relaxed on blankets and beach chairs. We spent most weekends together with family and friends. I knew that running my own business would siphon a lot more of my energy and time from family, but I could not calculate just how much. All I knew was I wanted more than a steady job with weekends off.

I swallowed hard and made the pricey reservation for one night in Houston, thinking that I would fly in, get some sleep, meet with Mr. Fisher the next morning and head back to Hampton Roads that afternoon. I spent several days honing my presentation, hoping I wasn't being some naïve goofball about to get scoffed at by some fancy billionaire. Whatever the result, I figured I would learn a few lessons and make some knew contacts.

I arrived at Armada Petroleum for my eight o'clock appointment. Mr. Fisher's receptionist pleasantly greeted me and I took a seat. My suit was pressed, my plans in a briefcase and my pitch rehearsed. After an hour passed, the receptionist apologized. An emergency had come up that needed Mr. Fisher's attention. Another hour and a half passed, and another apology from the receptionist.

I went to lunch, returned and waited some more. Another hour, and then another; still no Jim Fisher. By then, mild irritation swelled into full-blown anger. I began thinking that this was some sort of ruse, that I was some kind of sucker being jerked around and snickered at behind closed doors. What in the hell was I thinking. I had already had to rebook my return flight and knew that I would have to spend more money—that I didn't have—for another night at the swanky Whitehall.

I kept thinking about storming from Fisher's waiting area and leaving him a curt message. But something told me to stay. I kept telling myself to be patient. I am already here for another night, I thought, so I might as well ride this out. If I've been duped, another hour won't escalate my humiliation.

At about four o'clock, a slight, impeccably dressed man

with a Howard Hughes-like thin mustache and slick black hair emerged. Jim Fisher was courtly and soft-spoken, a slight man just as others had described. An apologetic Mr. Fisher told me to call him Jim as we entered through the double doors into his office. The view of downtown Houston below was expansive. My eyes darted from oil paintings on the walls to lustrous wood paneling and cabinets, to an oval conference table, to the panorama outside the windows. Jim sat behind an ornately carved desk that I would later learn cost sixty thousand dollars, more than the price of my first house. I had never seen such a richly appointed office. I tried not to look awestruck, but I doubt that I succeeded.

I stayed calm, but was anxious to pitch my plan just as I had rehearsed. I had blueprints, plats and appraisals spread out on the desk, but Jim seemed only mildly interested. He politely looked at maps, blueprints and cost figures. He listened without interrupting, asking only a few very basic questions about my proposal. My twenty minutes were up, and I wasn't feeling optimistic. I really felt I needed to sell Jim on the concept, to make him see the potential.

Once the formality ended, Jim told me to relax. He wanted to know about me, not my plan. He had already done his homework on the economics. He wanted to know about my family, my parents, where I was raised and went to school. He asked me about my time with Dun & Bradstreet and experience with Eastern International. We talked about my association with Nitze-Stagen and others in New York financial circles.

At one point, Jim asked where I bought my suit. A Portsmouth department store, I told him. "We need to do something about your clothes," he said with a slight grin. In recalling our first meeting years later, Jim said this about me: "This guy was a real salesman, and he dressed like one."

Jim talked about the Texas business culture that afternoon. It was high-risk, high-reward and fast-paced. In Texas, you took a man on his word, even when millions of dollars were at stake. Jim clearly wanted to make sure I deserved his trust. Jim and I talked and laughed that afternoon for nearly an hour and a half. I still wasn't sure Jim liked my business plan, but he seemed genuinely interested in me. At the very least, I figured I had made a friend and had a rare glimpse at big-time success. He was unlike anyone I had ever encountered.

Jim told me to sit tight while he made a call. He summoned the person on the other end of the line to his office. Not long afterward, Ken Griffin, Jim's chief finance guy, showed up. Ken had a check for me and wanted to know who to make it out to. He told me to deposit the money in my business account and wanted to know the name of my company. I meekly admitted that I didn't have a company, let alone a name for it or anything other than a personal checking account. Ken smiled and told me to take the check anyway and to fill it out and deposit it as soon as I incorporated.

Our deal was pretty straightforward: Armada Petroleum would invest seventy-five percent in our venture and I would cover the rest. Our ownership split would be the same. I would run the business and, assuming we were making money, Jim's company would continue to finance the bulk of the operations.

Before he sent me on my way that afternoon, Jim told me that he didn't know whether my business plan would work. What I do know, he said, is that "I believe that you believe your plan will work." He said he had a good feeling about me and that he had learned after many years in the speculative oil business to trust his "gut" about people. "I want to take a chance on you," Jim said. "I have a gut feeling, my boy, that you're going to make me money. In Texas, we go a lot on gut."

I flew back the next morning, astonished. Inside the pocket of my department store suit was a check for two and a half million made out to no one. These men, strangers really, who I had met less than a day ago, gave a blank check to some kid in his twenties who wanted to buy land in a Navy community they knew very little about. That check was soon deposited into the business account of newly formed Armada Hoffler.

Chapter VII
The New Kids in Town

"Doing the impossible only takes longer."

Jim gave me about two hundred thousand dollars more than I needed to buy the Greenbrier land and hotel site. He wisely surmised that I would need the extra cash as seed money to form and run Armada Hoffler. He was right, of course. I would need an office, at least a couple of staffers, supplies and an expense account.

Driving my 1965 Ford, I pulled up to a drive-thru window at a local United Bank branch and handed the teller the check and deposit slip for two and a half million. Her routine customer service smile morphed into a bug-eyed stare when she saw the amount. "Is this a joke?" she asked. She nervously asked me if I would wait a few minutes. I watched through the teller's window as the checked passed through several hands, presumably up the chain of command as phone calls were made. The check was good, of course, and I was in business.

It wouldn't be long before I would be chauffeuring clients around, so I needed a decent car. I bought a blue Pontiac sedan with velour seats and moonroof for eleven thousand. It was my first new car. Next, I leased office space on the third floor of a bland but functional office building that was almost within eyesight of the one hundred acres we now owned in Greenbrier. It had a small reception area, a couple of offices and a conference room. My office was the fanciest, with diagonal cedar slats on the wall—nice, but a far cry from what I had seen in Houston.

I hired three people: first was Beverly Browning, an associate from Eastern International. She was great with logistics and would be my office manager. Next came John Cote as operations manager, and finally my longtime friend Rick Burnell, who had since left Dun & Bradstreet and was working for a regional Xerox Corp. office in sales.

As with just about any start-up, everybody wore several hats and we all filled in for each other. John reviewed leases, contracts, expenses, hired subcontractors and got our warehouse and offices built. Rick was charged with finding tenants, identifying new clients and, eventually, hiring sales and marketing staff. Beverly did everything else, including keeping us three boys in line and on time. It was Beverly and I who worked shoulder to shoulder at my dining room table on our business plan just days after returning from Houston. She found the office space and helped me incorporate. She, like John and Rick, was upbeat, unflappable and extremely bright.

I met John while at Eastern International. He had been in the same office building, working for a company called Systems Management, a federal contractor that kept track of student loans and analyzed contracts between agencies and their vendors. John graduated from The University of Southern

Mississippi and served two years as an Army intelligence officer and then as a commercial loan officer with Virginia National Bank after that. John and I had similar backgrounds. His dad worked in the Norfolk Naval Shipyard and he was raised in a blue-collar neighborhood. He was sharp, easygoing and clearly very comfortable with the finance and legalese. Above all, he was trustworthy. John and I had become friends while I was with Eastern International, and we often went out for a meal or a couple of beers. It was over lunch that I convinced John to join my start-up company. Next came Rick, who had been at Xerox and embraced an opportunity to help his Churchland friend build an organization. Rick was a skilled marketer, a good listener, a nice guy and above all, loyal.

From the start, I was the engine. I wanted to get moving quickly and always looked for ways to make things happen rather than mull reasons why they could not. John would say that when it came to my enthusiasm, "The glass wasn't just half full, it overflowed." Rick called my zealous optimism, "contagious."

It was apparent to me from the outset that, above all else, I had to believe in our plan and myself to make the others feel the same. I always focused on what we could do or how to overcome obstacles. We didn't walk away from problems; we navigated through them.

To succeed in business, you need a solid game plan, a talented team to work with and a bit of luck. Perhaps most important is good timing. It's as cliché as any business adage but still valid. I admit that my timing for launching Armada Hoffler was mostly a sweet coincidence. Ronald Reagan shifted the political tide back toward restoring the military. Even before he took the oath of office, Congress got the message and started pumping money back into the armed services. President Reagan inherited what in today's dollars would have been a four hundred and forty-four billion dollar defense budget and jacked it up to five hundred and eighty billion. The Navy got a proportional slice of the pie, and there were lots of contractors anxious to help the service spend it.

When I was still with Eastern International, I had met an executive with CACI, a company that builds military bases. The Navy hired the firm to assist with its Saudi Naval Expansion Program and CACI needed warehouse space, lots of it, to store everything from toilets to electrical fixtures. Before we even razed the old whorehouse hotel on Diamond Springs Road, CACI signed a lease for three warehouses and office space we would build there. Those leases were money in the bank, enabling us to get financing and generate cash to do more projects.

Other big-name defense contractors were lining up as well to supply the Navy, and we were ready to accommodate: Wang Laboratories, AT&T, Litton Industries, Hewlett Packard and Sperry. We saw the wave coming and rushed to build warehouses on speculation, nervously confident that we could quickly fill them with tenants. We did better than any of us— even I—imagined.

In addition to the defense boom, the overall economy was poised to heat up as the crest of the wave of baby boomers was about to hit. The oldest baby boomer was age thirty-four and had been putting off buying a house through much of the 1970s. Now, they were raising kids and coming out in force to buy houses and furniture, clothes and cars. That was adrenaline for businesses, which began hiring, and as a result, needed more office space.

The federal government also stoked the burn for buildings with the Economic Recovery Tax Act of 1981. The law significantly cut capital gains and ordinary income tax rates. The best part of it for us was that the act allowed investors to depreciate a building over fifteen years instead of forty, which had been the standard. This Accelerated Cost Recovery System, reverently referred to as ACRS, made commercial buildings great investments rather than simply a practical need. The law was an example of how government can goose economic growth.

We caught the economic wave right at its break, riding it like a surfer tucked into a perfect curl. In eight months, we did two million, seven hundred thousand dollars in sales and leases. We were able to return to Fisher his initial investment, plus a quarter million profit in our first year. By our second year we had forty million dollars' worth of real estate under construction or lease. The profit to Fisher was a relatively small number for the behemoth Armada Petroleum but a startlingly fast return on investment, nonetheless. Jim became increasingly confident in his small but growing Hampton Roads investment.

With Fisher backing us, we had a great advantage over smaller real estate firms and even the bigger players out of Norfolk. They needed commercial banks to get projects financed, which takes lots of time and paperwork. We, on the other hand, had our own bank, Armada Petroleum. If we needed cash to build or buy more land, we would call down to Houston. We called it "oil money" in our office, a term of endearment. Knowing we had that level of support emboldened us and allowed us to almost immediately become a major developer.

The Diamond Springs project had been a stellar success and on May 13, 1981, we opened the first phase of Greenbrier Industrial & Office Park, the first of twenty buildings planned for our one hundred acres. My crew and I were energized and fearless. Like gamblers on a winning streak, we doubled up on the next bet, racing to stay ahead of competitors in the market and to ride the wave as long as it would carry us.

Our lives were exciting and fast paced. For me, Armada Hoffler became my obsession. I worked six days—and six nights—a week. This was not lost on my wife. Saturdays were particularly hard on her because I was often on a business trip, meeting with the marketing staff or taking clients fishing. Mary Jo would say that I was gone so often, our next door neighbor didn't know she had a husband. I did try to set aside Sundays as our family day, but growing the business siphoned nearly all of my attention.

After the close of regular business hours, my colleagues and I often shifted venues to a nearby restaurant for drinks and dinner. There, work discussions continued, which often morphed into chats about kids, family and personal challenges. For some of us, the overlap between business and personal matters became almost indistinguishable. We worked together, ate together and even vacationed as a group.

At our first company Christmas party, there were just eight of us, the four Armada Hoffler employees and their spouses. By the next year, we had more than two dozen. We continued to add staff to keep pace with our growth, quickly outgrowing our first office suite, then a second, before deciding to build our own headquarters in the Greenbrier corporate park. It would be a six-story building, the tallest private office building in the city.

Often, we would evaluate a prospective employee on how well that person mixed in social settings after the formal interviewing ended. We wanted people who, first and foremost, were smart, but we also wanted them to be fun, look sharp and have can-do outlooks.

I make no apologies for the fact that we often hired attractive people, especially our marketing staff. Attractive people usually get more access to clients. That was as much a reality when we started in business as it is now. Rick and I saw it countless times. Decision makers and CEOs were simply more inclined toward people, especially women, who were well-spoken, intelligent and who looked good. That didn't mean everyone needed to be a magazine cover girl or that they should act or dress provocatively. But in general, it did mean that representatives of our company were well attired, physically fit, pleasant to be around and social. That was true of the men in the company as well and of our support staff. Our administrative assistants, receptionists, finance specialists and other office workers were all expected to personify our culture. Some of our earlier business associates joked that they wanted to come to Armada Hoffler headquarters to see who we hired recently. Mary Jo often said that a lot of those women went to work for Armada Hoffler to find a husband.

One huge litmus test for me was how prospective employees—and their spouses—treated others. I would routinely take job prospects to dinner, mainly to see how they behaved when relaxed and to see how they treated the waitstaff. I have always admired waiters, waitresses, bartenders, hostesses and valets. Their jobs are hard and take great personal skill to do well. They deserve to be treated with the same respect as those making a six-figure income. Those who condescend to working class people are, in my view, elitists. They would probably treat subordinates or work colleagues just as poorly. To my chagrin, we have had to sever ties with staffers over the years who treated support staff, administrative assistants and others in our company poorly. Being disrespectful to others is, in my view, unprofessional and unacceptable.

There were several job prospects that did not get hired at Armada Hoffler because they were dismissive or rude to those serving us drinks or dinner. I also walked away from a business deal or two for the same reason. I tried to take the long view about building our business relationships.

Deals were starting to flow like a creek after a rainstorm. Our primary markets, Chesapeake, Virginia Beach and Hampton, were growing as quickly as the Navy's budget. Between 1980 and 1990, the number of Beach residents exploded from about two hundred and sixty thousand to almost four hundred thousand. Neighboring Chesapeake popped to more than one hundred and fifty thousand residents. Greenbrier, our home turf, became the epicenter of commercial growth in Chesapeake, attracting a regional shopping mall, strip malls, hotels and offices.

We were in the right place at the right time with the right product. It's hard to say now how much of our early success was luck. One thing I am certain of is that we hustled, took lots of risks and seized the moment. We enjoyed being the new kids in town and saw ourselves as the underdogs.

I was always looking for ways to inject confidence into our staff. We were a lot younger than our competitors, for one, and many of our newest employees had no experience in commercial real estate. I remember thinking about this when watching the movie "Rocky III" shortly after its release in 1982. Rocky was the nice guy who by sheer grit and hard work beat those who were bigger, meaner and more ring savvy. That plot and the movie's "Eye of the Tiger" soundtrack by the rock band Survivor got me fired up. We didn't have a TV in our office then, but I rented one that could play movies and had it set up in our small conference room. I required all Armada Hoffler staffers to watch "Rocky III" together.

Until we busted onto the scene, commercial real estate and development in the region was dominated by a few old-line companies with deep ties to the local banks and law firms of Norfolk. Among them were Harvey Lindsay, Goodman Segar Hogan, and S.L. Nusbaum, all top-flight firms that helped to bring some signature developments to the region. In our view, these firms and their founders deserved our respect but not deference. I remember going to a meeting in Norfolk where our firm and another were vying to renovate a historic but abandoned beer warehouse. The building had some unique issues because of the thickness of its walls. We came in with a very inspired plan but received a cool response. I was standing in an elevator with the founder of the competing real estate firm following a meeting. The old guard executive told me that, "Your day will come, but you'll have to wait your turn." I wasn't waiting for anyone.

We would grow Armada Hoffler not by copying the old masters but with new approaches to an old game. Companies were getting more aggressive with sales. Instead of waiting for customers to come calling or for referrals, marketing and sales managers of innovators like Xerox were unleashing waves of attractive, bright young salespeople to go find business. Rick had been one of those folks when he joined Xerox after leaving Dun & Bradstreet. At Xerox, salespeople were like advance scouts. Their job was to bring leads back to camp, or if they were really good, bring a prospect with them. The young ones would then hand off to two-and three-feathered chiefs who would negotiate terms and close the deals. That would be our culture as well.

Sales agents in many older-school real estate firms were paid primarily on commission. That made it hard to maintain talent in some companies and contributed to high turnover. As commissioned employees, the salespeople were essentially independent agents working more for themselves. In our view, that system created an inherent conflict of loyalty. Rick and I decided from the start that our agents would be salaried employees with benefits. Their success, job security and pay would, as a result, be linked to the prosperity of Armada Hoffler.

We also ditched the term "sales" agent. Our people would be marketers, implying that they would be promoting and growing the company, not just leasing office space. We paid them thirty-to fifty-thousand dollars in salary, and in return they were expected to follow what we called the ten-to-four rule, something Rick copied from his days at Xerox. It meant that our marketers were expected to be in the field from ten in the morning until four in the afternoon, checking in on clients and finding new ones to lease space.

Before our marketers were unleashed, we schooled them, sometimes up to six months, on construction and building design. We wanted our representatives to know about the thickness of walls, insulation and heating and cooling systems. We wanted them to be prepared when peppered with questions about one of our buildings. Another tactic was to put our marketers on-site, not in some distant corporate office at a desk waiting for a phone call. When a property was under construction, our agents would sometimes work from a trailer not far from the hardhats and architects. Once a building was completed, they worked from an office on-site to show around prospective tenants and to make sure the building was being properly managed. We expected our marketers to be experts on the properties they were hired to lease.

One of our training tools was a game we called "Mr. Prospect." I would pretend to be a potential client, and our marketers had to interview me to try and discern my business needs. We wanted our marketers to first understand a client's business before offering space or lease terms. That required some quick thinking and subtle but probing questions.

The banter became a fun but very competitive drill. Marketing associates critiqued each other's performance. More than once, an associate who fumbled stormed from the conference training room, frustrated and embarrassed. One guy almost quit on the spot because he thought I had intentionally made him look foolish. After blowing off steam, he came back to work. Lesson learned.

Rick also grilled our marketers, holding meetings each

week to review their lists of prospects and to make certain they were prepared when they hit the streets. And the staff did just that. They literally knocked on doors to solicit businesses that might want to relocate. They enticed companies with offers of more expansive or attractive office space at competitive per-square-foot pricing. If a tenant had a complaint about parking, they offered a location with plenty of parking spaces. If they were concerned about energy costs, we talked to them about the density of our insulation.

This approach is now SOP in the office leasing trade, but in the 1980s, many firms took a more passive tact by working together and then splitting commissions or by simply advertising their services or properties in newspapers, magazines or with signs in windows announcing available space. Many of the companies also worked on referral. If they didn't have a suitable building, the commercial firm down the road might. This quid pro quo worked fine if you were already part of the "good ol' boy" network. But we were on the outside looking in. Plus, we wanted to build our own network of clients and associates, and we wanted to lease "our" space.

Armada Hoffler crashed the party by landing major clients that included Federal Express, Sperry and AT&T. We also had dozens of smaller companies, mostly defense subcontractors. In less than four years, we built and leased more than one million square feet of office and industrial space worth twenty-five million dollars.

Economic growth is like a chain reaction. Companies that set up shop need other companies to provide them with supplies or services. Companies like FedEx were part of the food chain and so were we. We bought land with special tax incentives in airports and industrial parks. We knew those locations would grow because they had the support of Virginia Beach, Norfolk and Chesapeake officials. We helped to recruit to Hampton

Roads new companies, which meant more jobs, which bring more residents who need homes, which spurs the housing construction, which creates more households needing clothes and groceries, which creates the need for more retail space, and so on. Economists call this the multiplier effect. At Armada Hoffler, we were an integral part of that multiplier, especially in Chesapeake. Like the city and the region, we were rolling. In our first couple of years, I would tell my colleagues we were on the runway about to lift off and head for the clouds.

The buzz about our company started hitting a high pitch. We no longer had to recruit people to join us; they were coming to us in droves. Beverly would advertise for a marketing agent and get five hundred applicants. Those already on staff tended to stay with us. I am certain not everyone was happy all of the time. But from my vantage point, I saw a culture of camaraderie that made work fun and where our workers felt supported. There was a lot of laughing, teasing and partying in those early days that bonded us as a staff. We had parties for everything. We'd celebrate when we landed a deal, celebrate again when it broke ground and have a party finale when it opened.

When you spend that much time with people, you grow close. I helped or advised many individuals struggling with personal issues or career decisions. If someone wanted to move on to advance, we would help them. That was true of people at the top as well as our support staff.

For me, our culture was about loyalty. I gave a lot of it but expected it in return. Loyalty meant being honest. Somebody could screw up, but they needed to accept responsibility, let their bosses know immediately and do all they could to fix the problem. People at Armada Hoffler weren't fired for making mistakes; but if they lied, they were out. And if they had a gripe, I wanted to hear about it first.

Chapter VIII
Flying solo

"Many have mistaken my politeness as weakness.
But there is another side to me when
I have been betrayed."

My old mentor from Churchland, restaurant owner Eddie Speers, was serving his second term as a Chesapeake councilman in the early 1980s back when Chesapeake wasn't much on anyone's radar. Norfolk, as usual, and Virginia Beach got most of the attention from the local newspapers, TV stations and politicians. In fact, it was rare for a person seeking statewide office to even make campaign stops in Chesapeake.

At the time, the city didn't have much of an economic development office or budget to court new business. Armada Hoffler helped fill that void. Eddie and several of his council peers started informally calling me to see what we were up to and then dropping by our office for regular chats about what projects we had in the pipeline, what businesses we were recruiting and who the city might wish to pursue. These discussions got to a point where all or most members of the city council would meet informally at my office. Decisions were never made, nor promises. These were informational chats, a neutral place where city officials could brainstorm ideas or get background information on a possible business prospect for the city or other development proposals.

It was at a barbeque in 1981 that I befriended Gerald L. Baliles, a highly respected and courtly Virginia Democrat serving as the state's attorney general. Gerry cared deeply about social issues but also had a common sense view of business. He was neither harsh nor a demagogue and always a man of his word. I was drawn to him not because of his party affiliation, but because I liked the man. I enthusiastically supported him a few years later when he successfully ran for governor. Gerry repaid the favor many times over by attending a couple of key Chesapeake groundbreaking ceremonies for projects spearheaded by Armada Hoffler. Gerry would help get Douglas Wilder elected lieutenant governor of Virginia. Four years later, Doug would become the nation's first African-American governor. Gerry also introduced me to other lofty politicians.

My name started showing up as a significant campaign contributor to state and local politicians. Business competitors started griping that Armada Hoffler had an unfair advantage because of its political ties. The local media printed stories about private meetings between Chesapeake leaders and me, stories that were partly true but sensationalized and obviously intended to be inflammatory. No doubt the Norfolk newspaper sold a few extra copies by taking shots at me and my company. What amazed me was how my critics hid behind anonymity, criticizing me in the newspaper without disclosing their names. The most cynical of them would say that Chesapeake leaders were in the pocket of that developer, Dan Hoffler.

The truth is that city officials sought me out for advice. There were no deals cut, no promises made. City officials didn't ask me to bless or condemn a project. They did, however, seek my input and sometimes asked me to help them puzzle through a tricky issue concerning the city's growth. They asked me how much support a project might get in Richmond, whether it was one the governor or key legislators might back, whether the companies considering Chesapeake would be good for the city. I was more of a resource to the city than an influence peddler. I did want the council and its staff to be unified so that worthwhile corporate suitors wouldn't be scared off by political carping and fractured leadership.

On several occasions, members on council had disagreements. Just as with my business, I thought it best that officials share a common vision and try and settle differences amicably and with consensus instead of blasting each other in the press. One newspaper story said, in a headline nonetheless, that I handpicked Chesapeake's mayor. I still laugh about that. My only role was to bring together, in private, the two councilmen vying for the job. I encouraged them to settle their personal disputes and unify the entire council. This is what I told a newspaper reporter who asked me about the meeting: "I hear all of this stuff about kingmaker and I tell you it's a bunch of bull." It *was* a bunch of bull.

I was getting a crash course in the petty nature of politics and the power of perception. The news media, I discovered, can be like a trial lawyer stringing together a sequence of facts that seem to point to a conclusion. Another lawyer in the same case links another series of facts and arrives at yet another explanation. The facts presented on each side are accurate but the conclusions are misleading.

You can't control the direction news people take a story, just as you can't control which facts reporters elect to publish or omit. I soon learned there's no point getting frustrated by the process, because as seasoned politicians know, it's part of the game. I learned early on that the best play, when it comes to newshounds, is to give them the facts to chew on and then hope they have the honesty and intelligence to weigh them fairly. Just as with business people, lawyers and tradesmen, I have found some in the news business more trustworthy and intelligent than others.

Despite the scrutiny, I remained politically active, mostly because I was genuinely interested in public affairs and because it was good for business. There were more barbeques, more political fundraisers, more private dinners. I was also feeling the tug from my corporate sponsor, Jim Fisher. Occasional trips to Houston to report on our progress had become more frequent and personal. Jim took a real interest in me and showed increasing confidence in my ability. We had quickly gone beyond mentor and student. He trusted me so deeply with business and personal matters that I sometimes felt like a son to Jim.

Jim wanted me at Armada Petroleum board meetings or to sit in on key discussions about oil deals and investments unrelated to real estate development. I would sit quietly until Jim asked me to chime in. After a meeting ended, he would ask my opinion of certain individuals.

At one point, Jim wanted me to help the company sell an oil refinery. On a plane ride to Houston, I struck up a conversation with a businessman who, as luck would have it, happened to be in the refining business. By the time the plane landed, we had a deal roughed out. Within sixty days the refinery was sold. Jim was shocked and delighted, which provoked him to draw me even more deeply into the oil business. Jim exchanged my stake in Armada Hoffler for shares of Armada Petroleum. My personal wealth had suddenly surged. It was clear that I was being groomed.

Jim frequently flew to New York City for meetings, to shop or for entertainment. He would often pick up the phone and ask me immediately to fly into the city to join him. His calls always sounded urgent and important, so almost every time I was summoned, I'd drop everything to meet with him. I remember one such call when Jim said he needed to see me right away. He always stayed at the New York Helmsley on East 42nd Street in Manhattan, and as always, he booked a room there for me. When I arrived that day, I checked in and a hotel receptionist told me to immediately go to Tiffany's to meet Mr. Fisher. It was pouring rain and I arrived at the store soaking wet and slightly concerned.

"Come here, my boy," Jim said as I entered the store. "What do you think of this?" A saleswoman showed me a bracelet studded with gems. I was dazzled. What was this about? I thought. I politely told him the bracelet was beautiful, that his wife would love it. Then he said, "What about this?" He showed me a matching necklace. "Beautiful," I said again. He asked the price for both. The clerk said three hundred and twenty thousand. "Wrap 'em up," Jim replied.

The store manager told Jim an escort would accompany him to ensure he made it back safely to the hotel. Jim insisted that wouldn't be necessary. "The blood of anyone who tries to take this package will be on my boots," he said as we left.

Being around Jim exposed me to the finest cars, clothes, hotels, restaurants and jewelry. I was still a Portsmouth kid used to fried chicken, department store clothes and American cars, but I was learning how to appreciate the finer things and how to conduct myself around those who live in those upper echelons.

During one of my first trips to Geneva, I checked into yet

another swanky hotel Jim stayed at each time he traveled there. Once again, there was a message waiting. I was given the address of a tailor—Jim's tailor—and told to see the man immediately. My instructions were to buy a suit, a sports jacket and an extra pair of slacks. I was dressing better than I had on that first trip to Houston, but apparently still not meeting Jim's standards.

The tailor anticipated my arrival and was ready. He diligently measured me and selected fabric. When we were through, I asked him how much all of this would cost. I nearly choked when said more than two thousand dollars. "Can we do something cheaper," I asked. The tailor was firm. "This is what Mr. Fisher instructed me to do."

On yet another Geneva trip, I was reminded of my roots. Jim and I had met with a couple of business associates at an exclusive French restaurant. The waiter, who spoke French, took my order first. Wanting to impress my colleagues, I made an attempt to place my order in French, drawing on language classes I had taken in high school. As I spoke, the waiter chuckled smugly and said something to Jim and the others in his native tongue. Everyone at the table laughed but me.

After dinner, I asked Jim what was so funny. He grinned. The waiter said that I sounded like a French Gomer Pyle. Waitstaffs in nearly all high-brow European restaurants speak English, Jim said. "Stick with English, my boy."

Jim was extremely sharp-witted. Despite his extravagance, he never drank alcohol. His beverage was Perrier. I liked beer, the cheap stuff, and still do. Jim could not teach me much about fine wine, but he did give me an appreciation for watches, exclusive brand names like Patek Philippe and Cartier. Rolexes were just fine by me but too pedestrian for Jim. They had become commonplace in America. On my trips to Geneva, I would always make time to shop for a Rolex. I started giving them as gifts to my company executives. The gift of a watch was more personal than a bonus check. It was a daily reminder of my gratitude and a symbol of their success. More than once, tears welled in the eyes of those who received a Rolex.

I was quickly gaining a reputation for being ostentatious. I smoked fancy cigars, wore tailored suits and drove German luxury cars. I knew how that played in conservative Hampton Roads and how some of my rivals described me. Frankly, I didn't care. It they wanted to drive a Chevy that was their choice. A lot of people with money came from wealthy families. They grew up with vacation homes on the Outer Banks and country club memberships. None of that had ever been within reach for my family but now it was. I didn't drive a Mercedes to show off; I simply wanted the experience of owning one. I was like a kid in a candy store who never tasted chocolate. I was going to buy the best for myself and share it with my friends and colleagues.

I bought a large fishing boat and built a home on Hatteras Island. I loved to fish and often invited others along. If the vacation house wasn't occupied, I'd invite a friend or colleague to use it. If I was going to dinner locally or a Broadway show, I took guests. It wasn't about flouting wealth; it was about enjoying it. Jim Fisher showed me how to do that.

The oil business had once again shifted. The boom years were history. Federal regulators made it more difficult to freely trade crude and there was a ton of supply on the market from nearly a decade of aggressive drilling. Energy conservation was also part of the country's politics. American drivers were buying fuel-efficient Asian imports. I was starting to get an uneasy feeling.

I called Jim one morning after we had been together about three years and told him I was coming to Houston. We needed to talk. I was uncomfortable that so much of my wealth was tied up in Armada Petroleum. I wanted to sell back my shares in the parent company. When I entered Jim's office, he said, "I know why you're here." He was disappointed in my decision, but empathetic. I also explained that I needed to spend more time in Virginia with Armada Hoffler. We were growing fast and the business needed more of my attention.

John Cote started noticing that it was taking longer to get cash infusions from our parent oil company. Until then, Houston quickly obliged if we needed money. When we sold a building or mortgaged one that was leased, we sent cash to Armada Petroleum, and when we needed cash to buy another plot of land or to build, Fisher and his crew reciprocated. We had always got what we needed with a phone call. Suddenly, Houston started asking us for more money and returning less. Our cash pipeline was drying up.

Armada Petroleum bought back some of my stock but not all. I had done very well personally, but I worried about the ultimate fate of Armada Hoffler. Jim and his partners could sell us or all of Armada Petroleum for that matter, meaning we would go to new owners. Or, if our parent company went bust, Armada Hoffler could be dragged down with it. The worst-case scenario was about to happen.

Federal regulators started bringing charges against oil traders for misrepresenting their less expensive domestic crude as higher-priced imported oil. Refiners and their lawyers called the charges bogus. Domestic producers were essentially being forced to subsidize the high cost of imported oil. It was a complex, some would say vague system that criminalized what had been accepted pricing practices. Armada Petroleum got entangled in that legal web.

At the same time, some of the company's investments soured. The oil spigots had been running wide open and now there was an oil glut. As quickly as they jumped into the oil game, many independents were shutting down their drilling rigs. Oil stock prices plunged as companies filed for bankruptcy or simply walked away from unprofitable wells and refineries. The rise and fall of companies moved at lightning speed. The stock price of one company Jim had been associated with spiked from a dollar and a quarter in 1982 to almost fourteen dollars in 1983. That same company was in bankruptcy negotiations a year later, and its stock was worthless.

In the midst of federal indictments and an unraveling oil business, Jim cashed out of Armada Petroleum and the United States. He moved to Geneva and started a successful global consulting firm. In his wake was a bankrupt Armada Petroleum, which still owned Armada Hoffler. I wanted my company back, and I needed help.

A bright young lawyer named A. Russell Kirk had handled much of Armada Hoffler's financial matters in our first few years. He specialized in creating financing that used industrial revenue bonds or other complex blends of private and public funding. I had known Russ since we were boys growing up in Churchland, and I admired his success. Russ was a year ahead of me in school but we had many of the same teachers, classes and friends. His father, Arthur A. Kirk, was a well-regarded Portsmouth physician and philanthropist. Russ and I had lots in common. We were both preppy, straight-laced and business minded. One difference, however, was that Russ did really well in school. Russ attended the University of Virginia, "the University," and studied law at Washington and Lee, one of the state's premier—and most politically conservative—private universities.

Russ was interested in business from the start. He considered getting an MBA but decided a law degree gave him more flexibility. Russ went to work for Norfolk-based Kaufman & Canoles, which would become one of the region's most prestigious and powerful law firms. In less than two years, Russ became the youngest member of the firm to make partner, practicing precisely the kind of law he had hoped. He was making a lot of money with the firm, had great connections and was a highly skilled negotiator.

Russ was structuring most of my deals and by 1983 was intimately familiar with Armada Hoffler's trajectory. He became an adjunct of my company, a great sounding board, and one of my closest friends. I wanted to formalize that relationship. I confided in Russ the troubles with Armada Petroleum and wanted his advice on a rescue plan for my company. I wanted control of Armada Hoffler, but much of my wealth remained tied up in the stock of the parent company. At the time, Armada Hoffler also had a lot of paper debt because of the mortgages and bonds used to finance our various buildings. Most of our cash had either been reinvested or had been siphoned by Armada Petroleum.

A company run by an investor named Bill Nathan had purchased Armada Petroleum and was taking it out of bankruptcy. He was an oil industry investor with little interest in commercial real estate. On paper, Armada Hoffler showed a lot. We got wind that Bill had been considering just letting Armada Hoffler fold. A couple of us had spoken with Bill and, best we could tell, he seemed to like us. What was clear was his indifference toward commercial real estate.

Russ combed over our books and felt confident that Armada Hoffler could prosper on its own with a small cash infusion and by getting permanent financing on some of our construction loans. Most of our buildings were more than ninety percent leased and those that we were building had promising tenants. The Hampton Roads economy was still chugging at a fast clip, especially in our corporate hometown. Russ had some money of his own to invest and borrowed some from his dad and others. It was a risky choice for the young lawyer, one that would mean a hefty pay cut. Dr. Kirk supported his son's decision to leave the law firm, telling him, "You will either do exceptionally well, or you can go broke." Russ assured his dad he would not go broke.

Russ and I met with Bill Nathan on familiar turf, the Helmsley in New York. Bill was happy to see us and to unload the commercial real estate arm of bankrupt Armada. Russ and Bill scratched out a deal, writing it on a yellow legal pad while we sat at the hotel bar. Basically, we would assume all of the company's debt and I would exchange my remaining stock in the oil company for control of Armada Hoffler. Russ kicked in some cash and co-signed some loans, receiving a seventeen percent stake in Armada Hoffler and the title of company president. I controlled the remainder. We didn't hear from Bill for more than a month and started to worry. We were relieved to finally receive the paperwork and close the deal. Russ and I were now joined at the hip financially and personally. Armada Hoffler was ours.

I have often been asked what my key strength is as a business leader. The answer is the same now as it was in the first years of Armada Hoffler: Recognize what you don't know, acknowledge your weaknesses, and surround yourself with people who can fill those voids. In Russ I had a keen analytical mind and someone I could completely trust. Russ was a straight shooter, a cut-to-the-chase businessman with a lawyer's critical eye. I was the dreamer and Russ was the pragmatist; I focused on the big picture and Russ made certain all of the details were in place. I was the high school principal who set the agenda, and Russ was the vice principal who made sure rules were followed. We were a classic good cop, bad cop team.

Throughout our four decades in business together, Russ has been a quiet force behind our success. He's been a master at avoiding bad deals and putting us in lots of good ones. He's often the guy with his forehead in his hand, leaning over excruciatingly detailed documents on his desk. He's the guy more often than not combing a contract line by line and conducting hardball negotiations with other eagle-eyed lawyers and bankers. I have often said "You can't teach judgment and you can't fix stupid." Russ's judgment has been impeccable and his business acumen inspiring. Together we created a culture and enlivened it with people who would fill other voids, people excited about the company and who knew how to enjoy the ride. We were about making money and having fun.

By the mid-1980s we were at full stride, growing so fast that it became hard to manage Armada Hoffler as one company. We were developing land, constructing buildings and leasing them, plus drifting into other tangential deals that looked like moneymakers. We had built ourselves a new corporate headquarters in Greenbrier, replete with signature-rounded corners, brick façade, flowing staircases and window-wrapped atriums. We wanted our building, like others we created, to be full of light and open. We wanted our workers to feel like they were in a living room instead of the salt mines. We did lots of tile, glass, fountains and plants. We also added lots of new faces. Our company had grown so many branches and was hiring so rapidly that I sometimes lost track of who was who.

I require all employees to wear a triangular lapel pin with the company's logo. It is meant to symbolize loyalty, integrity and trust. I was riding the elevator to my office and noticed that the young man standing next to me was without his pin. I had seen the man several times before, but his named escaped me. He stood dumbfounded as I admonished him for not wearing the pin. When I reached my office, I immediately asked my assistant to find out the man's name. Turns out the guy worked for another company with offices in the building. I avoided riding the elevator for the next several months.

Chapter IX
Bigger and Better

*"I have critics, but I don't think anyone would say that
I don't remember where I came from."*

With the "oil days" behind me, I could focus exclusively
on our business. If I wasn't in a meeting or at lunch or dinner,
I tried to be in the field surveying our projects or mingling with
staff. I wanted to remain more than just a nameplate. I had
learned early on the importance of staying connected to the
people who get things done—the tradesmen on a construction
site, the administrative assistants, mid-level managers. If you
become aloof, the rank and file no longer work for you; they
work for a paycheck.

It was a rainy, cold spring day when I visited a job site to
check on progress. I had heard some of our subcontractors were
having trouble excavating a site for offices and warehouses.
The men were cold and wet and standing around a burn

barrel sipping coffee to get warm. I walked up unannounced, wearing a trench coat. The men didn't notice me—or at least they pretended not to. They were grumbling about the work conditions, weather and the difficulty of the job. From the home office we were pressing the contractors to meet a deadline so we could start building. My name came up. Hoffler, one of the men said, needs to "come down from his ivory tower." There were a few other disparaging remarks that cast me as an elitist. I never mentioned anything about that moment to the crew's bosses or my people. I am grateful to those men for teaching me a lesson: Stay connected. If work crews were dealing with problems, I wanted to know.

It was tough to get to every job site while our company was expanding through the mid-1980s. But when I did visit, I always made it a point to speak with the hardhats. Most of them were subcontractors—excavators, masons, electricians, carpenters, plumbers, laborers. Their bosses or crew leaders would often squirm when they saw me coming. I wanted to know if the worker bees had the materials or equipment needed. Were there any problems? When I found some, I acted immediately. I'd return to the office, summon a few key people and tell them to bring a pad and pen. Our focus at these fix-it meetings was to find solutions. Those responsible could be dealt with later. Assigning blame never fixed anything, and there was usually plenty to go around when something did go wrong.

Construction sites, when run properly, can be a like a ballet. One phase of the dance segues seamlessly into the next. But if there is a break in the chain, everyone downstream is knocked off balance like dominoes. Building materials on the site must be ready, waiting and of the right mix. If the window installers show up and the windows are the wrong size, that means the building can't be closed and kept dry, which means the floor and tile workers can't start, which creates moving delays for tenants. This can become more than just a chain reaction of inconvenience. Poorly managed sites can take longer to build and have a lot of do-overs. Lost time and materials cost money. It also pisses off the subcontractors and their tradesmen who show up on a job ready to work but then can't because of some problem that may have nothing to do with them.

At Armada Hoffler, we often worked off of very slim profit margins and tight construction schedules to remain competitive. One way we protected ourselves early on was to stick with a predictable building size and style. Many of our first office buildings were six floors and about one hundred thousand square feet. We softened our office exteriors with rounded corners and columns. Our large signature windows were recessed about three inches, which could save us as much as one hundred thousand dollars on steel and other materials. We used heavier insulation, washable wall coverings and high quality roofing to enhance energy efficiency and maintenance. Our lobbies had high-grade marble floors that gave a warm feeling but withstood heavy use too.

Competitors criticized our buildings as cookie-cutter and said that companies wanting Class-A office space would turn away. Nonetheless, we wooed them by providing custom lighting and other architectural extras that, while appealing, didn't require us to significantly alter our business designs. We could also complete a building in six months. Our business model was built on speed. Our construction division had become so efficient that we could build a big box store for the Price Club in ninety days.

The pile driver behind our aggressive construction schedules was Louis Haddad. This imposing man is a gentle giant with a warm demeanor but a laser-like business focus. Lou, a member of Mensa, the oldest high-IQ society in the world, was a great construction site choreographer and an imaginative

Lou Haddad, Russ Kirk and I celebrating at a company party.

problem solver. Even as a guy in his twenties, Lou had a cool head and was a natural collaborator. He fixed problems instead of inflaming them with personality clashes. Once, when work halted on a site because the ground was too wet, Lou sent in the company helicopter to hover ten feet overhead, using the wind from the blades to dry off the ground below.

Lou is not an academic, although he could have been. He left the classrooms at the University of Maryland and landed instead in the hardhat world of construction. That was an odd turn for a kid with Lou's pedigree. The first American wave of Lou's family came from Syria and settled in a small coal mining and steel mill town in western Pennsylvania. Lou's dad was a highly decorated World War II Marine who fought in Iwo Jima and earned a field commission for his heroism. He went to college on the GI Bill, made a career in the secretive United States State Department and served as a liaison for President Reagan.

Lou didn't fully embrace his dad's "God and country" devotion and decided on a different path. As a kid growing up in Potomac, Maryland, he had marveled at the scale of huge buildings under construction in Washington and its Maryland suburbs. Job sites interested him more than classrooms and textbooks. He left college in his sophomore year, not really sure what would be next. That changed when he discovered Harkins Builders, a large commercial construction company behind some of the structures Lou had admired. Harkins had a management program that groomed young apprentices to become construction site superintendents. Lou received an interview but was told that he didn't qualify for the program. He immediately asked what job he could get. They offered him a job as a laborer.

On his first day, Lou reported to a townhouse construction site. Water was seeping into the basement, and Lou was told to dig a trench around the outside basement wall to find the leak. He had to continue shoveling until he hit the gravel bed beneath the foundation walls. It was August and steamy hot. Blisters soon formed on his hands. His back hurt, and he was soaked from sweat. It was almost noon, and Lou had been shoveling a trench line for hours but had not yet hit gravel. Sore and disheartened, Lou decided that construction might not be his calling after all. He decided to gut it out until lunch and then quit. Within minutes of break time, Lou's shovel found gravel. Buoyed, he completed the trench, found the source of water and reported to his bosses. They couldn't believe he had finished the job so soon.

From that point forward, Lou did everything he could to be noticed. First of all, he dressed like a superintendent instead of a laborer, wearing pressed khakis and clean shirts. He showed up early each day, volunteering to work weekends or OT when needed, and, as Lou puts it "worked harder and faster than anyone else." Lou did get noticed and after about a year of busting his hump with a shovel, he was enrolled in Harkins' apprentice program, which was considered the gold standard of construction management training.

Lou quickly moved up the ranks at Harkins. As an assistant

superintendent, he managed various aspects of a construction project, such as crews laying concrete and installing bricks. As a superintendent, he was responsible for all aspects of construction, which on a big job could be orchestrating one thousand workers coming and going in waves as needed. The project manager, usually a white-collar executive, is next on the food chain.

A gaping void at Armada Hoffler had been that no one in leadership had a construction background. I was a marketing guy and knew very little about the fine points of construction or site management, and Russ was a lawyer. Our team was super strong on land development, leasing and finance, but often clueless on the fine points of getting something built.

Lou had been assigned by his company to help manage a construction project in Hampton Roads. He was single at the time and met up after work for beers with some of the project's subcontractors. One of our Armada Hoffler executives had heard about Lou through the grapevine and decided he had to meet him. We were only building Armada Hoffler projects at the time, so our construction arm was very small. Lou was flattered when we approached him about joining us but politely declined. We were too small time.

About a year or so later, he was sent to Hampton Roads again to manage another Harkins job. Lou had remained on our radar but still showed little interest in joining Armada Hoffler. Finally, in the fall of 1984, his wife, Mary, convinced him to at least interview with us as a courtesy. Lou capitulated, figuring he would "just get it over with."

"At the time, Armada Hoffler was all about marketing," Lou would later say about that initial meeting. "What impressed me was that these guys envisioned what they wanted to become and acted like they were already there."

Lou was just twenty-six at the time and figured that he

was young enough to recover professionally if Armada Hoffler flopped. Lou started with us as a superintendent but only had a chance to get one building under his belt before we promoted him to project manager. In February of 1987, Lou, then just twenty-eight, was named president of the entire construction division. Lou's ascent continued over the next decade, landing him in the chief executive's chair for the entire company.

Lou made us realize that construction was more than a necessary evil—it could be highly profitable. Lou persuaded us that we could make money constructing buildings for other companies. I was cautious at first, telling him that he could accept outside work as long as Armada Hoffler buildings took priority.

Lou was unabashed about his expectations and set a clear path for his project managers and superintendents. One of his credos: Keep subcontractors happy by staying on schedule. Lou knew from his experience at Harkins that subcontractors who made money on a project would almost always send their best crews to work with that builder again. Poorly managed construction sites costs subs time, and therefore, money. So, builders with lousy superintendents or poorly planned workflow gained a bad reputation and as a result would be assigned the worst crews by subcontractors. It was a self-perpetuating cycle of success or failure. If a sub or a worker groused, Lou gently but firmly told them that Armada Hoffler pays "above-market salaries and demands above-market work." He was demanding without being demeaning—a tall, heavy-bearded regular guy in the field but a shrewd executive behind a desk.

Under Lou, our construction arm flourished and soon would be the most profitable division of the company. Lou's approach was to avoid the cutthroat and costly public bidding process. It often forced construction companies to work on margins so slim that they could easily lose money, which many did. Instead, Lou and his crew sought out companies or institutions that needed new facilities, such as a warehouse, wholesale club or assembly plants, but had no interest or skill at construction. Our earliest clients included Hampton University, Hills Brothers Coffee, Sam's Club and Price Club, which became Costco.

By mid-decade, we were firing on all cylinders. Our leasing and development arms thrived as Rick Burnell and his marketers signed scores of tenants. We had expanded into finance and insurance and veered into residential development. Home building and sales were outside of our comfort zone but seemed to dovetail with our experience in land development and construction. In June 1986, we launched our sixth division, Armada/Hoffler Residential Real Estate. Business textbooks call this "vertical integration." For us, it was more simply an extension of serving our business clients. A lot of the bigger companies moving to our buildings needed help finding housing for their workers.

Some came from outside the region, and some of our deals lured employers from more crowded and older urban centers in the region. Our biggest score was moving eight hundred General Service Administration workers from six World War II barracks at the region's large Navy base, to new offices in Chesapeake's industrial park in the heart of the Greenbrier section. The city had hoped the location, called the Volvo site, would have more industrial clients. Instead, we convinced leaders that the land would be perfect for retail and offices. We contracted with the city to develop two hundred of the five hundred acres.

For the GSA and other companies that followed, we became their one-stop real estate shop. Our commercial teams would set them up with offices and our residential agents would help their workers find housing. We invested a quarter of a million dollars to get the housing company rolling and expected to have as many as forty sales agents. Part of their job would be to market lots and sell houses in two Chesapeake subdivisions we owned, Plantation Lakes and Oak Grove Lakes.

We reorganized the company to keep pace with growth. Each arm was a separate entity under the Armada Hoffler umbrella, which seemed to keep sprouting new appendages. We bought an interest in a Miami company that sold long distance telephone service to businesses, and we even tried to open a mobile home park. I personally had a stake in several small businesses, such as a travel agency and restaurants. I liked betting on people who impressed me.

I had been around a lot of lawyers, but few had wowed me as much John W. Brown. I was first introduced to John at a social event in the early 1980s. He was from the North, but came South to attend college and then law school. After a stint as an assistant Commonwealth's attorney, John went into private practice with another lawyer. John had that rare combination of being very bright but very down to earth. He could relate to anyone. He was as comfortable with Harvard-educated businessmen as blue-collar workers. He was a great listener and storyteller, someone others liked being around.

John was doing fairly well in his law practice, but I knew he was capable of much more. One evening I showed up unannounced at his home in Chesapeake. I was very blunt with John and his wife, Donna. "John, you might think you're rich making one hundred and fifty thousand dollars a year, but trust me, I know you can do a lot better. Stop thinking of your work as a job, and start thinking like a businessman."

I persuaded John to start his own firm and set him up with an office and all of the work he could handle. He was tapped by politicians to serve on several boards and in 2008 was appointed as a Chesapeake Circuit Court judge, receiving the endorsement of key players in both political parties.

John had a bird's-eye view of some of my company's best and most dicey real estate deals. One that we still roll our eyes over was forced on us.

Sometimes you partner with others to protect your own interest. That's fairly common in the development game. And that's what happened with the Salt Ponds development on the James River in Hampton, Virginia. We were the primary builder of the project, which was to be a high-end residential community wrapped by a swanky marina. Initial plans called for six hundred condos on one end of the development and single-family houses on the other. There would be a basin, boathouses, restaurants and lots of piers and docks for boats. It would be a waterfront showcase. We were pretty deep into the project when the developer ran out of money. In lieu of the one million we were owed, we took an ownership stake and quickly scaled the development back to sixty condos with hopes of selling it out and moving our cash elsewhere. We lost millions on the project, which became an albatross and a harbinger. The commercial real estate sizzle began to cool. Our bank lenders, especially Nations Bank, stuck with us and allowed us to negotiate more favorable terms on ailing projects, such as Salt Ponds. But in general, new financing started drying up, along with demand.

Just as the federal government had goosed our industry in the beginning of the decade, it chopped our legs from under us with new rules. Reagan, now in his second term, significantly cut income taxes. But as part of his 1986 reforms, he also killed the accelerated depreciation rates on commercial buildings and various tax write-offs on rental and commercial properties. Suddenly, offices, warehouses and condominiums no longer were tax havens, which made them less profitable and less of a sure bet. Businesses that owned their offices and warehouses also got stung by cuts to the depreciation allowances. They responded by putting the brakes on expansion.

Russ, Rick and other key executives in the company noticed that occupancy rates on many buildings were kept artificially high. Leasing agents were giving tenants huge incentives, including free rent for a year or at deep discounts. Demand for new buildings had also dried up. The tide was about to turn on us pretty quickly, and Russ and the others were getting nervous. We owned dozens of buildings with large mortgages. We started negotiating new loan terms, stretching payments or asking for lower interest rates. Mainstream banks and other lenders were starting to get nervous, making it difficult to refinance. The high-fives we had shared at so many of our executive meetings now turned to handwringing.

Each year we had a corporate retreat and in 1989 we met at the Tides Inn on the Rappahannock River. Before the partners meeting, Russ said he needed to speak with me in private. The two of us spoke just about every day, so I knew this was serious. Through the decade, I was the dreamer and Russ was the pragmatist. I was the good cop, the popular high school principal; Russ was the bad cop, the vice principal kids would see when they were in trouble.

"Dan, we need to sell the helicopter. We can't afford it. It's costing us a half a million a year," Russ said. He added that we may need to lay off employees, something we had never done. Our permanent workforce had grown to more than two hundred, plus we had legions of subcontractors, vendors and associates. We needed to shift into survival mode, and it was time to share the news with our team.

Girding for what we believed was an impending crash consumed us for months. We held formal strategy sessions at least twice a week and had countless discussions with clients and lenders, most of whom were showing signs of fiscal stress or at least worry. Our least vulnerable division was the construction company headed by Lou, which was generating close to two hundred million dollars a year. It was a mostly pay-as-you-go operation that threw off cash and kept people employed.

Our most shaky divisions owned real estate. Our housing arm had been doing well. We owned three subdivisions and had twenty agents who sold thirty million dollars in housing in 1989 alone. Despite that, we still carried lots of inventory. Most of our income and debt came from the cadre of office buildings and other commercial properties on the books. If leasing rates continued to decline on several of our largest properties, we would be in the red. It was time to cash out, even if it meant unloading some land and buildings at a loss. We needed a buyer, and fast.

We were familiar with the international commercial real estate behemoth Jones Lang Wootton. The company had gobbled up billions of dollars in real estate during the boom years and owned trophy office buildings in New York, Chicago and overseas. Jones Lang had done well with properties in secondary markets such as Hampton Roads and liked the market for its steady growth and huge military presence. We owned three dozen commercial buildings and Jones Lang was big enough to swallow our entire portfolio in one gulp, sparing us from the excruciating task of selling our assets piecemeal, which could take years. Had we waited to sell or been delayed, we might have hit the rocks and sunk. Within a year, the real estate market crashed, sparking a wave of bank failures and the country's eighth recession since World War II.

Point Farm in Eastville, Virginia.

Chapter X
Point Farm

*"Always remember to treat everyone well on your
way up because you might meet them again on
your way down."*

The recession forced me to tap the brakes. For nearly a
decade, I had been running full speed, building a company that
went from four people to more than two hundred; entertaining,
mixing with politicians, bankers and notables; bouncing from
state to state and between the U.S. and Europe for business and

pleasure. My twenty-four-seven lifestyle exacerbated an already strained marriage, which had emotionally exhausted Mary Jo and me. We had two wonderful daughters who bound us together, but our connection frayed and though I was conflicted about ending my marriage—I loved my kids and cared for Mary Jo—we divorced by the end of the tumultuous decade.

My reputation for flamboyance had grown along with my company's success, and the press was now covering us aggressively. My affiliations with several big-name politicians, including two Virginia governors, also put me in the spotlight. I enjoyed the attention and my growing influence in business circles, but that recognition also kindled my desire for quiet time.

I had always loved solitude. That's probably why fishing, and later hunting, appealed so strongly to me. They were an escape from concrete, elevators, meetings and phone calls. The outdoors allowed me to smell the earth, the ocean and bays and relax my mind. Among my favorite haunts was Virginia's Lower Eastern Shore. I often fished in the Chesapeake Bay and set my boat in for gas or bait at the Shore's Cape Charles. The quaint little town seemed like it was in a time warp, with a general store, some antique shops, Victorian houses and a few taverns. Local law enforcers and other Shore notables often gathered in a room over the hardware store for drinks. Most everyone was on a first-name basis and knew the names of each other's kids. The Shore is only about twenty miles from bustling Hampton Roads, but it is truly like being in another time zone.

The Shore is connected to Virginia Beach by the Chesapeake Bay Bridge-Tunnel, a two-tunnel toll bridge that allows Navy and cargo ships to shuttle between the Bay and Atlantic. The toll is steep, now twelve dollars to cross one way. It's a fabulous drive of almost eighteen miles over water but one that can be treacherous in high winds. One accident can shut the Bridge-

Tunnel for hours. It's a spectacular, but impractical, daily commute.

Before the road was built, the Lower Shore was a dead end. The only way across was by boat or airplane. Those who lived on the Shore generally stayed on the Shore. It was a community of farmers and fishermen with a few B&Bs and motels for travelers. Many of the families along this narrowing peninsula have roots in the seventeenth century.

I had purchased a small farm on the Shore, mostly for hunting. My interests started shifting from fishing to wing shooting. I especially liked pursuing waterfowl, and the Shore was nothing short of a duck-hunting haven. Geese poured into the grain fields and surrounding creeks. Ducks funneling down the Atlantic Flyway on their way south gathered in the salt marshes of the ocean and the web of creeks and ponds on the Bayside. Quail hunting was spectacular. Many Shore farmers were willing conservationists, making sure they kept rows of thick vegetation, called hedge rows, between farm fields to provide quail, rabbits and other small game with a place to hide from hawks, fox and other predators.

A politician from the Shore, who I had met socially, told me about a historic piece of property that was being sold. It was known locally as Point Farm, a spectacular peninsula of about one hundred and twenty acres wrapped by Cherrystone Creek and a half-mile of Bay frontage. The land was being farmed and came with a historic house. The property itself had deeds and land records dating to 1620.

The state parks and recreation division wanted to buy Point Farm and make it part of a five-hundred-acre park that would potentially draw millions of visitors to its beaches and historic buildings. However, the locals, including the politician who reached out to me, were opposed because of the traffic a state park would bring. Shore residents, especially those with land and money, covet solitude. The thought of gawking tourists motoring along their quiet, almost private roads and splashing on their beaches did not sit well.

One day, I asked Bobby Doak, a pilot for Armada Hoffler, to check out Point Farm for me. Bobby wasn't just hired help; he had helped me get through my divorce with Mary Jo and had become a confidant and spiritual advisor. Though I didn't belong to a church, Bobby, a deeply religious, unassuming man who had once been a gospel singer, didn't judge me. We shared the view that the way a person lives and treats others is the ultimate measure of a person, not whether they attend a church or adhere to the rules of a certain religion.

Bobby and his wife, Carol, who was my administrative assistant at the time, made the trip to Point Farm while I was traveling and spent hours walking the property. Bobby called me with a warning: "Dan, don't go see the property unless you're going to buy it. I know you, and I know when you see it you're going to want it."

Bobby did, in fact, know we well. My enthusiasm sometimes got me in trouble and, once, almost got us killed. Bobby and I were riding in a newly delivered corporate helicopter with controls in each of the front seats. I grabbed the control stick and leaned it to one side to get a closer look at some intriguing land. Suddenly, we were flying sideways. "Dan! Let go of the controls. You're going to get us killed!" Bobby yelled as he averted what could have been a deadly mishap.

Bobby dropped me off and immediately took the helicopter back to its hangar. He had the passenger controls removed. He knew me well enough to know I would again cave in to the temptation to grab them. "Where are my controls?" I asked Bobby the next time I boarded the helicopter. "You're grounded," he said. That was fine with me. I used the space where the controls had been to keep beer when we flew.

A couple of days after a snowstorm, Bobby took Dad and I on a helicopter ride to check out Point Farm. The white fields below were bordered by the deep-blue water. Ducks were scattered in small groups feeding along the edges. There was no traffic on the narrow road leading to the glistening property. My dad and I were awestruck. The view was breathtaking, one of the most magnificent sights I had ever seen. Bobby was right. Dad and I smiled at each other and gazed below as the helicopter dipped down for a closer view.

I've always loved American history and Point Farm had a wellspring of it. The Lower Eastern Shore was Powhatan land when English setters first arrived. According to numerous historical accounts and folklore, a boy named Thomas Savage arrived on a resupply ship sent to Jamestown in 1608. Wanting to strengthen ties with Native Americans, colonialists sent Savage, who was thirteen, to live with the Powhatan on the Eastern Shore. In return, the tribe sent one of its own to live with the British. It's not known exactly where Savage lived, but some historians believed he resided, at least part time, on what is now Point Farm.

The boy was well-regarded by the Powhatan, learning their language and culture. After three years, he returned to the British colonies and helped negotiate trade with the Powhatan. The British king rewarded Savage with four thousand acres on the Shore that included what would eventually become Point Farm. Savage moved onto the property and was believed to be the first permanent white settler on Virginia's Eastern Shore. Savage's land holdings reached nearly nine thousand acres. Historical records show he received large swaths as payment for transporting English settlers to the New World.

Point Farm and much of the land surrounding it stayed in John Savage's family for nearly two centuries. The barely two lanes that end at the entrance of Point Farm are named Savage Neck Road. The family's land holdings were carved up with each succeeding generation. Brothers, uncles, offspring and widows were deeded portions of the property in wills or as payment, historical records show. By 1833, the core of John Savage's land had been whittled down to a little over six hundred acres. The succession of families that owned the Farm includes some of Virginia's most notable: Littleton, Stith, Parker, Nottingham, Floyd and Wescoat. One owner was George Yardley, the son of a Virginia governor. Rufus P. Custis bought Point Farm in 1927 for one thousand and five hundred dollars. During the Great Depression, he and scores of Eastern Shore farmers mortgaged their property with the Federal Land Bank. Many lost ownership because they couldn't pay off the debt. Custis and Point Farm survived.

Between 1939 and 1946, the Farm changed hands five times, eventually falling to George W. Ames who paid thirteen thousand for it. Ames kept the farm and lived there until he drowned in 1984. Local game warden Mike Caison, who I would later befriend, found Ames's body facedown on an oyster rock about three dozen yards from shore. Ames was not married, had no children and had been living with a younger man, John E. Norling.

Ames and two others decided to fetch some oysters from Cherry Stone Creek. It was late in the afternoon on a winter day. The three men paddled out about 200 yards from the farmhouse when the canoe tipped. The two guys with Ames were much younger and able to swim back to the shore. Mike was nearby when the emergency call came. He had a boat across the creek and quickly set out to start searching. The sun was almost down and the water cold. A Coast Guard helicopter beamed a light down on the water. Mike saw a silhouette on a rock just a few yards from where he was searching. The body was colorless and its lips were blue. Ames had apparently drowned and somehow washed up on the rock.

Ames had named Norling the heir of Point Farm. After a few years, Norling decided to sell it. Business partners and others told me I was crazy when they heard the price. Norling listed the farm for three and a quarter million, and we agreed to three and a half million. Friends laughed at my folly. "There's nothing up there." "Do you have to hunt to feed yourself?" "How big is the outhouse?" It was true. There wasn't much in Northampton County, the Shore's lower half, when I arrived. The county is among the state's poorest and most isolated. About three-quarters of the county is under water and only about thirteen thousand people inhabit the two hundred square miles of dry land.

I shrugged off the criticism as jest. Yes, I paid a big price for the farm, especially with a recession bearing down. But in my mind it was a unique piece of property unrivaled on the Eastern Seaboard. Things that are rare or extraordinary usually increase in value over time. I believed that to be true of Point Farm and the Eastern Shore in general. This spectacularly beautiful place was slowly being discovered by the outside world, and when the recession lifted, it would become an even more coveted destination, especially for baby boomer retirees.

Still, all of that seemed beside the point. I wasn't buying it as a short-term investment anyway. I had no interest in subdividing or developing it. In fact, that's precisely what I was escaping. No, Point Farm would be my sanctuary, a sort of Disneyland for hunting, fishing and horseback riding, with no lines, no noise, no traffic and privacy assured by the water surrounding it. The locals—at least some of them—were relieved when I bought the property, instead of the state. Word quickly spread that my only intention was to live there.

The farm was far enough away from the office and work but close enough to be in Hampton Roads when I was needed. In fact, I shuttled back and forth for a while in a helicopter, which no doubt kindled the criticism of me as a high-minded "come here." I soon learned that you didn't have to hunt to eat in Northampton County, but there weren't many options besides convenience stores and fast food. Hardee's chicken and light beer in aluminum cans would soon become a staple—and I loved it.

Owning the farm and improving it would occupy me during the drudgery of the recession. Between 1979 and 1989, Armada Hoffler built nearly three dozen major projects of our own. During the recession we would build just one. Thankfully, our construction division remained busy building for others, enabling us to keep most of our people on the payroll. As we rode out the economic storm, we watched with dismay as several other developers that were encumbered with debt, folded. Savings and loans were dropping like flies. S&Ls were specialized lenders that used federal backing to provide low-interest loans for residential and commercial real estate. To make money, many of these banks gambled on speculative real estate deals that paid big up-front loan origination fees and offered the potential for big returns. Developers like us took advantage of that enthusiasm, further inflating the already stretched real estate supply bubble. Fortunately, Virginia and our home region were spared the worst of the meltdown. But states like Texas, where speculative lending ran rampant, got creamed. Nationwide, half the S&L banks failed, bankrupting the federal fund that insured their loans and forcing Congress into a major bailout. Land and buildings from these failed lenders were being auctioned at pennies on the dollar, dragging down the values and prices of pretty much everything else. It was a great time to buy, but only if you had cash. And companies like mine were holding onto what little we had stockpiled.

The real estate industry turned to mud. Many of the lenders or investors we had done business with lost their jobs or companies. Real estate sales offices closed and companies merged. The strong gobbled up the weak. Office vacancy rates were nauseatingly high. In those days, you generally needed to keep about ninety percent of a building leased in order to make money on it. In our primary markets, buildings were running a quarter-to a third-empty. Businesses and individuals were lining up at bankruptcy court in droves to jettison bad debt and real estate holdings. It was a tough time to feel good about any aspect of the development business. Economists debated whether we were in a true recession, which to me seemed like a running bad joke. I didn't need a bunch of statistics to convince me. Times were tough. Russ, Lou and I did our best to keep spirits up at Armada Hoffler, but daily headlines trumpeting lending scandals, bailouts and foreclosures kept the mood dour.

The crisis was much bigger than us, and we could only hunker down and survive. I did my hunkering in duck blinds and tree stands on the Shore. I had moved into the eighteenth-century Savage house pretty much full time and was enjoying my rustic surroundings. The home was modest and needed a lot of work. For me, my hunting buddies and other friends, it was more like a clubhouse for grown boys. We tracked mud in through the side parlor. We put our feet up on the dining room table, grilled fresh fish, chicken or burgers on the patio. We drank beer from aluminum cans and steamed clams scooped from the creek a few yards away.

I noticed almost immediately how relaxed people became at the Farm. The isolation and laid-back atmosphere melted away the intensity of business and family for lots of friends and associates. Chatting over coffee after a morning shoot was engaging and jovial. Back in the 1980s, I did lots of entertaining on my various fishing boats. While most of my guests enjoyed going off Hatteras and into the Gulf Stream to hunt tuna, marlin or other trophy fish, those trips often left them feeling queasy. Boats can also be cramped and privacy limited, making business talk difficult. At Point Farm you could go for a walk or jog on the beach and not see anyone. And you could party all night and never worry about driving anywhere or embarrassing yourself.

I have more crazy stories about escapades at Point Farm than hair on a monkey's arm. Once, after a few beers, I took some guests for a tour in my new all-terrain vehicle. Riding with me were a railroad executive, a political and business heavyweight from the Shore, and a lofty state official who had just arrived for a weekend of bird hunting. We came to one of several ponds on the property, and I wanted show them how my new toy could float. Let's just say my approach was off. The machine skidded down the incline and capsized. We wound up chest-deep in water.

We've had several close calls, lots of hangovers and a book's worth of regrettable jokes. Guests were often an eclectic mix of Shore farmers and other locals whom I had come to know, Armada Hoffler business associates, close friends, politicians, celebrities, authors and professional athletes. My guests had immunity to get into as much fun as they could stand. Friends started calling Point Farm "Danny Land." An old girlfriend even had a sign made with that name and nailed it to a tree near the Farm entrance. We didn't have our own set of laws in Danny Land, but we did have a code, the same one touted in Las Vegas: "What happens here stays here." Those who showed a lack of discretion or who were intrusive or rude were not invited back. That rarely happened.

I found most of the locals to be friendly and eager to share a beer. Many were fairly new arrivals to the Shore, like me. I'd see them at Hardee's or one of the local bars or gas stations and made it a point to chat it up and remember their names.

Some weren't so friendly. A few of the landed gentry, those from families that had been on the Shore several generations, ignored me or invitations to meet. They were wary of the slick developer from the "other side" of the water. I heard through others that some of the Shore bluebloods were unhappy that people like me, outsiders with money, were moving in and buying up prime real estate. One notable warned one of my newfound friends to stay away from me. The rumor was that I made all of my money as a druglord. "Be careful with that guy. All that glitters isn't gold," my friend was warned. I shrugged off comments like that, just as I had when being snubbed by Norfolk's old guard.

Bird hunting soon became an obsession. On the Shore it's a tradition woven deeply in the culture and it spans generations. The Chesapeake Bay region has a rich history of waterfowling and of notorious characters who flouted game and fishing laws. Generations of locals made careers as commercial hunters, guides and decoy makers. On the Shore, kids often learn to shoot before they are taught to hit a baseball. The family dog is as likely to retrieve point birds as to fetch a stick. On the Shore, camouflage and knee-high rubber boots were not worn to make a fashion statement. Run-of-the-mill pump shotguns or older side-by-sides were as much tools as toys. Rich guys I knew with elite European double-guns couldn't match these local boys when it came to shooting. The Shore guys—and girls—stayed relaxed and pretended to be indifferent about whether they bagged a bird. But they did keep score quietly and showed dismay if they missed an easy mark. I was missing a lot when I first arrived. I could fish with the best of the locals, but shooting at this level was a new game that I embraced enthusiastically. I did what rich guys do: I got lessons and practiced—a lot. I was blessed with good hand-eye coordination and fortunate to have befriended a couple of guys who gave me lots of shooting tips and an education about wildlife. One of them was the local game warden.

I met Mike Caison not long after moving to the Shore. He was wary of me at first and politely sidestepped a couple of invitations by a neighbor to be introduced. Finally, he did come to the Farm for a visit. Mike was friendly and polite but no-nonsense when it came to enforcing hunting, fishing and trapping laws. He had been an Air Force brat, bouncing around with his family until his dad retired in nearby Hampton. As a young man, he saw a newspaper advertisement for a game warden, landed the job and was assigned as a rookie to rural Northampton County in 1976. In his first year, Mike issued two hundred and sixty citations. The year before, only about thirty had been written. Mike was not aiming to win a Mr. Congeniality contest among hunters. The Shore had been wide open for game law violators who were killing game out of season, ignoring bag limits and killing protected species. He dwelled in a fascinating but dangerous world where he routinely pursued violators carrying loaded weapons.

Mike and I became fast friends. I had an insatiable curiosity about hunting and conservation, and Mike knew all there was to know about game laws and wildlife on the Shore. He was also a damn fine shot. Mike and I went to a few sport shooting events to see the pros in action. As a result, I hired an instructor who, at the time, was ranked as one of the top sporting clay competitors in the world. Iowan Jon Kruger came to Point Farm and helped Mike and I with the layout of a five-stand sporting clay range that we were building next to a hovel I called the gun lodge. Jon drilled me in the mechanics of shotgun shooting, which consists of three steps: Move with the target, mount the gunstock to your shoulder and shoot through the target. "Move, mount, shoot" is a fast, fluid motion that is more like swinging a baseball bat or golf club than pointing a rifle. You have to get in front of a target and move through it.

I poured through cases of shotgun shells and clay targets, those black-and-orange saucers about four inches in diameter and about an inch thick. I learned to shoot the clay birds at varying speeds and angles. Mike and I also became certified sporting clay shooting instructors, mostly so we could properly teach others how to shoot safely and effectively. Many of my guests at the Farm had never handled a shotgun. Safety always came first, which meant never pointing a weapon—loaded or unloaded—at another person. Once a shell slides into the firing chamber, there is no room for error, so I would often stand beside guests, load one shell at a time and make sure they kept the barrel facing the shooting range.

Working on my shooting and teaching others became my singular passion. Once, golfing great Curtis Strange visited the Farm and offered to teach me how to play his game. I declined, mostly because Curtis was visiting to relax and shoot, not to give golf lessons. I started attending more competitive shooting events and entered a few myself. I even managed to place third in a field of several hundred shooters. Shotgun enthusiasts, I soon learned, were an eclectic group that ranged from plumbers to European nobles. It didn't matter in the field or on a sporting clay course if someone wore overalls or Armani suits to work. A great shot was a great shot; a good guy was a good guy; and assholes were just that.

Among the good guys was King Howington, builder and developer who lived north of Atlanta and who loved to shoot. King had a beautiful farm and was showing me and a friend around the property. King had a stable and several horses on the property. His daughter was into competitive English-style riding. The girl's riding coach kept her horse at King's and she was preparing to ride when we stopped by the stable. The young woman, in her mid-twenties, was a stunning beauty. She was about five feet seven inches tall, lean, blond and blue-eyed. She wore a fitted tank top, riding pants and knee-high leather jumping boots. She looked like she had stepped out of the pages of a glossy fashion magazine.

King introduced me to Melissa Hyde, who was grooming her horse and adjusting the saddle. After some small talk, Melissa rode off to warm-up her horse. After King finished giving the tour, I drifted back toward the riding area to watch Melissa work on her routine. Her horse was a monster, but she gracefully maneuvered over and around a series of jumps. By then, I owned a few horses that I kept at Point Farm, but they were pleasure horses, not the sleek, ripped beasts that can bounce over four-foot hurdles and then glide as if running on air. I didn't know much about "eventing," but I knew enough about riding to appreciate the athleticism of courage needed to control these high-strung animals. I could have watched Melissa all afternoon.

King told me a bit about her: recently divorced from a European guy who had been her riding coach and business partner; attending college; a top competitor who trained with equestrian Olympic coaches; coach of his daughter's equestrian team; owner of a business that boards and imports jumpers. At the time, Melissa was pretty content to be single and was very busy pursuing an economics degree and running her businesses. She got asked on lots of dates, but usually declined. She was polite but somewhat aloof when we were introduced at the stable. She also didn't acknowledge me much when I returned to watch her ride later that day. None of that discouraged me. A couple of days after returning to Virginia, I called King for a favor: Would he ask Melissa if she would consider meeting me for a date? "I think that's a question Dan Hoffler should be asking me—not you," Melissa told King.

Virginia Governor Doug Wilder and I had by then become companions. I came to know Doug when he was the state's lieutenant governor and running for the top job. I worked as treasurer for Doug's campaign, traveling with him, fundraising and hosting events. I liked his intelligence and spirited personality and was thrilled when Lawrence Douglas Wilder became Virginia's first governor of African descent and the first in the nation since Reconstruction. I was with Doug when the results of the race came in on that November evening in 1989. He won by less than one half of a percent, a margin so slim it prompted a recount.

Doug was often criticized, even by fellow Democrats, for being too independent minded. I actually liked that about him. He stuck to his guns and followed his own moral compass. Although he grew up in Richmond, Virginia, a bastion of conservatism, Doug was a middle-of-the-road Democrat. He had learned to work with conservatives while in the state Senate and often advocated positions that made both parties squirm. I lived vicariously through Doug, getting a front seat to the allure of elected leadership and the backbiting pettiness and plotting between rivals. Virginia state politics had largely been a gentleman's club of lawyers and well-to-do cliques that frowned on those with a maverick streak or sharp words. Doug grew up outside of that bubble. One reason we bonded is because we both saw ourselves, at least to some degree, as outsiders.

It's hard to explain exactly why two people connect. One thing for sure is that there has to be mutual respect. Another is the way you see life. When asked about our friendship, Doug says, "We connected very well because we didn't allow or even entertain the idea that obstacles could stop us. We focused on how to get things done."

Doug and I were a lot different too. He thrived on being in the public eye; I liked playing possum. I didn't mix well with politicians because I couldn't talk the talk. But I could, as Doug says, "insinuate" myself into a conversation and then listen and study. I heard it said many times that "Dan is too nice of a guy" for politics. Yes, maybe on the surface. But Doug saw the other side of me as well. I could play hardball; I just didn't do it in front of a crowd. Doug and I had a saying: "Never pull a weapon out unless you intend to use it." I have to admit that on at least one occasion, Doug was my weapon.

Doug had been invited to speak at a conference in Atlanta, and I was looking for a reason to get back down there, so I offered to accompany him. I called Melissa to see if she would like to meet the governor after the speaking event. It was a thinly veiled excuse to see her again and to impress her. My friend Doug played along. I had arranged ahead of time to have Doug flown back to Virginia that afternoon. I would hang back and try my luck with Melissa. My plan worked. She would be heading home and offered to drop me off at a hotel where I booked a room. She said her vehicle was modest, but she didn't say how modest. She was driving a beat-up pick-up she used to pull horse trailers. Melissa seemed unruffled when the truck didn't start. She explained that it happened all the time and then got out and popped open the hood. She jiggled the battery cables, which seemed to do the trick. She laughed, and I rolled my eyes as we pulled away.

I asked Melissa if she would meet me for breakfast at the hotel the next morning before my flight back. When she showed up, there were several boxes in shopping bags in the chair beside her. She opened them one by one, giddy and surprised. I had gone shopping the night before and bought her a jacket, slacks and some shirts. Thankfully, I guessed her sizes right.

I thought about her nonstop and called her for a few weeks

at about the same time each day, usually early afternoon. One day I called to make certain she would be at home; I said I was having something delivered. Melissa figured it would be flowers. When she answered the knock on her door, a young man smiled and handed her a set of keys. In the driveway was a black Mercedes 500 convertible. "Mr. Hoffler said that this car should be more reliable. Would you mind giving me a ride to the airport? I need to catch a plane back to Virginia."

We started dating after that, and it wasn't too long afterward that Melissa moved onto Point Farm. She loved that I already owned horses and saw the great potential for building a stable and riding. She also loved the old farmhouse tucked in the shade up along the creek. Like me, she loved the outdoors and became enchanted with the Farm.

We spent our honeymoon in ducks blinds in Uruguay. Melissa took videos of our hunts and tried hunting too. We went horseback riding, ate great food and shopped. Shortly after our return, a four-legged wedding present was delivered to the Farm. The governor bought two purebred Gordon setter puppies that he named Desert Storm and Desert Shield, after the war in Iraq. He gave us Storm. The dog was gorgeous, with a wavy black coat and chestnut on his chest and muzzle. Doug knew I liked to bird hunt and thought the dog would be a good field companion. I soon realized that Storm, a friendly slobbery mass of energy, didn't like the sound of gunfire and didn't really figure out what to do when he smelled a bird. Storm was basically useless in the field.

Melissa tried to fix that. One afternoon, she loaded Storm into the front seat of her convertible and drove up the road to Stockley Kennels. The owner, Neil Lessard, bred, trained and hunted some of the finest bird dogs in the country. Neil's dogs, like most used in the field, are speedy athletes that can run full tilt for hours and then stop on a dime and freeze in place when they smell a bird. His dogs, usually English setters or pointers, have light, short coats that are mostly white to keep them from overheating. Storm was almost the opposite: big, dark as night and lumbering.

Neil wasn't quite sure how to react to the hot blonde in a black Mercedes pulling up on the gravel driveway with a dog in the front seat. Most of Neil's customers drive pick-ups or SUVs and haul their dogs around in travel crates. Without making guarantees, Neil said that he would work with Storm. After a month or so, Storm flunked out of bird dog school. The great thing was that Neil became a friend and hunting companion. He would often guide when I had a hunting party, showing up with some of his best dogs and taking us to farms with lots of birds. If I wanted to entertain a hunting novice, Neil would place some pen-raised pheasant or quail in a farm field and then allow our guest to shoot. Neil's dogs would go on point, allowing the shooter time to get into position.

We entertained lots of interesting personalities. Some of our guests came from money and showed up with leather gun cases, twenty thousand dollar shotguns, hunting knickers and wool caps—attire worn by British royalty. The locals, on the other hand, usually wore Carhartt, knee-high green rubber boots bought at the local hardware store, and they bought chain store shotguns or relics handed down through the family.

One very wealthy Virginia woman became indignant when Neil instructed her to kick a clump of field grass holding a pheasant. The dog was on point and the bird pinned. Neil explained that it's the shooter's job to kick up the bird. The woman, who had been on exclusive pheasant hunts on European estates, refused, saying that flushing a bird is the job of hired help. "Ma'am, on the Shore we flush our own birds," Neil quipped. We all laughed about it later over beers.

Locals barely missed a rising quail or duck pitching into decoys. They preferred hunting wild birds, which can blast off and be out of sight in seconds or dip and weave like a bat chasing bugs. Guests and novices often poured through boxes of shotgun shells trying to score, especially at early fall dove shoots. Sometimes, when their misses became embarrassing or they became frustrated, Neil or another skilled hunting friend or I would shoot at the same time as our guest and then give them credit for the kill. Our mantra at the Farm was for our guests to have fun, even though I often was accused of being a "game hog." We flashed grins at each other when guests bragged about the great shots they made. I was happy that they were happy.

We took lots of people horseback riding and carefully paired our guests with a proper mount. We always kept a few docile horses, ones that would barely trot no matter how hard you planted your heels in their side. We kept some fiery mounts too, for those bold and experienced enough to handle them. We did the same with fishing or jet skiing by always trying to put guests in situations they could handle and enjoy.

One of my most frequent guests was the governor. He liked to ride, shoot pool with me at the gun lodge, play poker or just hang out and talk. Everyone needs someone to talk to, and I had become one of those people for Doug.

Point Farm had quickly transformed from an outpost to a home and weekend retreat for guests. My oldest daughter, Sara, left boarding school at age twelve to live with us. My youngest daughter, Kristy, visited often and also eventually moved in. We were blessed to have Annie Bowers with us too. Annie had helped raise Sara and Kristy. My daughters and I considered her family. Annie was blunt and as protective of my girls and me as a bear over her cubs. She nourished them with food and advice. She was a stout lady with a big smile who didn't sugarcoat her feelings. If she liked someone, she loved them. Those she didn't care for were politely snubbed. I had dozens of people around me but few I trusted as much as Annie.

We quickly outgrew the eighteenth-century farmhouse. It was quaint but just too small. I thought about building a new home at the west end of the farm, closer to the "point" and the Bay. But Melissa loved the setting of the original Savage family house, which was tucked along the creek and near a shallow cove where ducks, geese and songbirds congregated. I built an apartment for Annie on top of a bay of garages next to the house. We then renovated the main house, stripping it down to its rough-hewn floor and wall studs and expanding it. We were careful to preserve the original façade and made certain the addition meshed perfectly. It was a beast of a project that cost more time and money then I had planned, but it turned out great. The renovations left us with six bedrooms and three stories, with open views of the creek. We also built a pool house that was really a party room and created a large stable and riding arena that also had an apartment. Between these buildings and the gun lodge, which had a loft, we could accommodate several guests—and we did, nearly every week. We were always entertaining or planning a party. We had a cornucopia of friends, a combination of Shore locals, high-ranking Navy officers, politicians, judges, business CEOs and my associates from Armada Hoffler.

My greatest skill as a business person had always been studying people and bringing them together. I made lots of introductions that ultimately resulted in political appointments, job offers or business deals. The governor appointed me to the boards of the state transportation commission and the University of Virginia. Some acquaintances became great friends.

While wing shooting was my first love, I quickly graduated into bigger game. The Shore was becoming thick with deer, once a rarity. Farmers had been shifting away from grains to soybeans and vegetables. The Shore became a giant salad bar that deer gorged on. But as they flourished, some bird populations, especially quail, declined. There were still plenty around, thankfully, in my first years on the Shore. Several local farmers, including my good friend Roger Buyrn, generously invited me and guests to help thin the burgeoning herd of deer. Roger, who lived across the creek, also invited us into some dynamite goose pits he built in his fields. We placed special guests, and sometimes their wives, in the best hunting stands and then walked through the woods to drive the deer toward them. Roger and his buddies picked up the game and took it to his farm, where, after the hunt, we butchered the animal into venison steaks and presented them to guests as gifts. We gave game to some poor local families too.

Like so many on the Shore, Roger spoke with authority about the environment, soils, water tables and conservation. Roger could also quote Longfellow or discuss in great detail the strategy behind a pivotal Civil War battle. He could fix a diesel motor, make his own lumber from trees on his land and turn hundreds of acres into mats of soybeans or cotton. He smoked a corncob pipe and sported mutton chops, a brimmed hat and long sleeves even in the summer. He also carried an old Parker side-by-side shotgun with double triggers and full choke barrels, a relic that most hunters would have mounted above a fireplace as a showpiece, but not a weapon of choice in the field. Roger often embarrassed others brandishing English shotguns with ornate checkering and walnut stocks or those with semi-automatics with gas-vented recoil that acted like a shock absorber. Roger's old Parker kicked like a mule. It was like firing a cannon. That's probably why Roger shot so efficiently. He would pull the trigger half again fewer times and wind up with half again more birds in his pouch.

Hunting, fishing and partying on the Shore was like being in a time warp. It felt like the middle of the twentieth century, not the end of it. That, I think, was the ultimate charm of Point Farm in the 1990s. It really was a place where boys could be boys, where you could shoot geese at daybreak, fish for blues or strippers in the afternoon or just chill out and watch heron work the shoreline or hawks snatch a varmint from a field and carry it off.

The Shore is a throwback in other ways as well. It's a community of haves and have-nots. Northampton County consistently ranks among the state's poorest areas. Tucked along the back roads are trailer parks, migrant farm housing and ramshackles that go back generations. There's not much quality employment, especially on the Lower Shore, so work can be scarce. Lots of younger people flee the Shore once they graduate high school. For many, the only other option is to wait on tables, tend bar or work at a fish house. But lots of young people do stick around. The Shore, locals say, gets in your blood. It didn't take long for me to understand why. Often, when I traveled for extended trips, even to remote and beautiful places in South America or Europe, I'd long to get back to Point Farm.

On any given weekend, Melissa and I might have a houseful of guests from several states and varying backgrounds. The common denominator for most, however, was a love of the outdoors and shooting. I always tried to match hunting partners based on personality and interests. Hunting can be social, or it can be very competitive. If you put two aggressive strangers in the same duck blind, for example, one will likely piss off the other. If you partner one person who is gabby and jocular with another who is silent and intense, chances are there will be some friction.

One universal rule, regardless of position or background, was that all of my hunting guests had to safely handle a weapon.

The careless or reckless would not be invited back. When you're messing with guns, you must be able to trust the people you're with. One of the most embarrassing moments for me was during a dove shoot on a field I owned not far from the Farm. One of my employees, a newly hired executive, brought an automatic rifle to the dove field. The guy walked down toward the creek and started unloading a flurry of rounds that sounded nothing like a single burst of shotgun fire. A judge, who was a very good friend, politely excused himself. Possessing and firing an automatic weapon under these circumstances was a federal offense, he said. The judge got in his vehicle and drove off. A couple of others also later complained about the guy and his cowboy shoot 'em-up antics. That employee was never invited to another one of my shoots and lasted less than a year at Armada Hoffler.

Mike Caison helped keep us on the straight and narrow. Mike often helped me organize a hunt, which meant all quests were properly licensed, that the shoot began after sunrise and ended before sunset. He was a stickler for safety and more than once admonished a guest who did something dangerous or stupid. Mike didn't discriminate, either. He once confronted a high-ranking military officer whose muzzle nearly blasted a fellow hunter standing in front of him. Most of the hunting mistakes I witnessed were just that, mistakes. In duck hunting, for example, there are lots of species that look very similar, especially when the light is low and they're swooping by. Even the most experienced wing shooter can misidentify a bird or its gender. It's happened to me.

As a game warden, Mike had lots of dangerous moments on the job that required a cool head and iron stomach. He would sneak up on poachers spotlighting deer at night or nab duck hunters illegally spreading corn around their blinds to lure birds. He took weapons away from men who had been drinking or who were using illegal ammunition. It was dangerous work. Like any law enforcer, he needed to use his judgment, knowing when to be harsh and when to use a mistake as a teaching moment.

Mike, Roger and three other friends had joined me on what would become one of many hunting trips to South America. We were in Uruguay about to embark on an afternoon dove shoot. Our guide shuttled us down a remote country road where we pulled off to the side and removed our shotguns from their cases. Suddenly, several military vehicles sped up and uniformed soldiers leaped out, pointing machine guns at us. The militia stood us shoulder-to-shoulder along the road's edge. Our guide was frantically speaking to them in Spanish as we stood stock-still.

Our shotguns were leaning against the van we had arrived in. Roger is not someone easily intimidated or cowed. He once challenged a rival to a duel. Thankfully, the other guy never showed up. Roger, who was standing next to Mike, whispered, "I think we can get to our guns if we move fast." Mike whispered back, "Roger, don't you move. They have machine guns." Thankfully, Roger held. It turns out that some notable had been assassinated in a nearby town and the police thought we were a posse of South American vigilantes on a stakeout waiting for the murderers to flee down this remote road. Our guide got the matter resolved but not until after about a half an hour of convincing. Once our nerves settled, we had lots of laughs over that story, which, like so many hunting stories, ripen with age.

Chapter XI
Politics

"If you're in politics, you'd better be prepared to
take a punch, because when it gets nasty,
you're gonna wind up bloody. Personally,
I was never cut out for it."

Early in my career, I learned that politics and business
are connected like muscle to bone. One doesn't move without
the other. Yes, business people or rich guys do give money to
political campaigns with the expectation of some quid pro quo,
but it has never, at least in my personal experience, been in any
way financially inappropriate or illegal. Neither my company
nor I have ever been handed a government contract because
we knew someone. Government jobs, at least when it comes
to construction, require competitive bidding. Companies that
participate usually cut their profit margin so slim just to win a
bid that they can ultimately wind up losing money. Big public

Former Virginia Governor L. Douglas Wilder and I

U.S. Senator Mark Warner and I

Valerie and I with Virginia Governor Bob McDonnell and his
daughter Jeanine

Valerie and I with former U.S. President Bill Clinton

Valerie and I with former Virginia Governor and U.S. Senator
George Allen and his wife, Susan

Hampton University
President Bill Harvey
and I

projects also can be a public relations headache. If there is a mistake or delay or something needs to be added or changed, local politicians may resort to handwringing, especially when TV and newspaper bloodhounds start howling about wasted taxpayer money and use phrases like "boondoggle." Another problem is that elections change the moods and people in charge. Politicians can get skittish around election time, shying away from anything at all controversial. You can also wind up with a slate of new leaders who have a different agenda. One mayor might be in favor of a proposal and the next might hate it. We've experienced that in a couple of communities. It's the prickly nature of business and politics.

In very general terms, most people in elected office are motivated the same as most everyone else: They're honest people with good intentions who want to get ahead in life but who sometimes act out of fear instead of being courageous. Some elected folks are publicity hounds and garner attention by being bombastic or outspoken. Others tread carefully, positioning themselves as courtly or reasoned or just straight-laced and squeaky clean. I have known governors of both personality types who exited the political stage bruised but accomplished.

I got my first up-close look at national-stage politics shortly after I partnered with Texas oilman Jim Fisher. An impressive retired Marine with high political ambitions had married the daughter of Lyndon B. Johnson, the powerful Texan who rose to become U.S. president. Then Lt. Governor Chuck Robb had the backing of Virginia Democrats who were trying to rebound from a string of losses to Republicans. Chuck was a fresh-faced moderate with a Bronze Star from his tour in Vietnam. He catapulted into celebrity when he married Lynda Bird on the White House lawn with President LBJ at his side. LBJ was popular with blacks and liberals, and Robb was acceptable to mainstream Democrats and some Republicans. Jim was interested in contributing to Robb's campaign for governor, in part because of the connection to the powerful Johnson family of Texas.

I arranged a meeting between Chuck and Jim at a restaurant in Portsmouth. It was cordial and resulted in Jim and I making a twenty-five thousand dollar financial pledge to support the rising star who had grown up in Alexandria, the Virginia suburb of Washington. I quickly discovered that once you donate a significant sum to one politician, others sniff you out like ants do sugar. Your phone starts ringing and lunch invitations pile up.

It was at a fundraiser for Chuck that I met Doug Wilder. Doug was the second in a troika of rising Democrats looking to recapture the Commonwealth's executive branch. Doug was the grandson of slaves, a Richmond-raised kid who grew up poor and black in a city that still celebrates its heritage with monuments to Confederate leaders.

Doug often talked about growing up in the shadows of Virginia's governor's mansion and historic capitol, which sit side by side on a hill overlooking the city. As a boy, city leaders and its voters paid almost as much homage to Jefferson Davis as Thomas Jefferson, both of who made history on that hill.

Wilder's parents paid homage as well. They picked the name Doug as a tribute to abolitionist Frederick Douglass. A love of history and a fire for learning burned in Doug. He attended Virginia Union University, a historically African-American school and, like Chuck Robb, earned a Bronze Star in combat. Doug returned from Korea an Army hero but wasn't allowed to study law in his home state because Virginia law schools didn't admit blacks in the late 1950s. Doug, instead, enrolled in historically black Howard University, not far up the road in Washington.

I liked Doug from the first day we met. The fundraiser for Robb was at a Chesapeake restaurant I had owned. I asked Doug how his finances were shaping up. When he told me, I said, "You need help." We laughed and knew we had lots of work to do and money to raise.

Doug was feisty and charismatic, with a big smile and a gentlemanly Virginia drawl. I think we saw a lot of ourselves in each other. We both rose from modest backgrounds and lacked the sterling pedigrees of typical Richmond power brokers. Just as I had started my own business, Doug established his own law firm, which gave him the freedom to pick and choose his political battles and legal cases. He wasn't a man accustomed to asking for permission to speak and was self-aware enough to realize he would have suffocated in the league of bowtie Richmond conservatives who ran the city and its biggest law firms.

Doug's political IQ was among the highest I had ever seen. He knew his base and how to artfully champion the social causes that motivated him without falling too far from the mainstream. The art of compromise, I was learning, really was more of an art of preparation. And everything in politics revolves around money. That much I knew. It takes tons to get elected and then pretty much every decision, once in office, is over how to spend it. Politics is like business in that way. Doug says it's "a people business" because it is "the people's business." It looked and sounded a lot like sales and marketing to me.

Doug used his appeal to set a series of firsts for African Americans in Virginia since Reconstruction: the first state senator, the first lieutenant governor. When he declared candidacy for the big job, I was the first person to contribute money to his campaign and became his finance director. I accompanied Doug on dozens of campaign stops and fundraisers, marveling at his flair and energy on the trail. He was getting a lot of attention as yet another Virginia Democrat with national potential.

A year earlier, Virginians rewarded Chuck Robb for a job well done as governor by sending him to the U.S. Senate, a contest he won with seventy-one percent of the vote. Chuck, the clean-cut retired Marine and centrist Democrat, was seen as presidential timber. Suddenly, he and Doug started to be presented in the media more as rivals than allies.

Doug felt that Chuck's support of him for governor was tepid. Chuck had won his race by a landslide in the fall of 1988 and Doug, who was in a very tight contest, had hoped to get a boost from those coattails. Doug let it slip out that he thought the senator could have been more supportive. The pundits, always drooling for new fodder, chomped. They fomented a so-called feud between Chuck and Doug, which, in my opinion, was exaggerated and inflamed by loose-lipped political aides to both men.

Doug took it all in stride. He realized—and told me many times— that taking licks from critics and in newspaper headlines simply comes with the turf of high office. "You can't win" in such situations, the governor said, so you just have to "grin and bear it." Stepping into a political controversy, he liked to say, is like stepping into quicksand. The more you thrash and panic, the deeper you sink.

Chuck Robb had definitely stepped into it and was flailing. His sterling reputation started getting battered after he was governor and while running for the Senate. Chuck had spent lots of time socializing in Virginia Beach. Political enemies spread the word that Chuck was a party boy seen with prostitutes and cocaine users. As the scandal unfolded, Chuck admitted that he had been at some Beach parties but adamantly denied involvement with drugs or prostitutes, allegations that were never substantiated.

Doug was on the campaign trail when the news of Chuck's problems hit the media. Doug knew a frenzy was building and that Chuck was in trouble. Doug and I discussed the implications for Chuck more than once. Everyone seemed to be talking about it. An amateur ham radio operator secretly, and illegally, recorded one of our cell phone chats. The guy made an audio tape that would remain a secret for two and a half years.

On the campaign trail, Doug never seemed to tire. He needed only a few hours of sleep to recharge. I remember fighting off heavy eyelids more than once while we bounced from fire hall, to school cafeteria, to church halls, to Rotary clubs, meeting new faces and building support. Governor Baliles assigned a state trooper to protect Doug during the campaign. That was an unusual precaution, but some worried that Doug's race might provoke an attack. Threats had come not only from bigoted whites but from blacks who thought Doug was too mainstream or hoity. Those around Doug seemed to worry about threats more than him.

Once, late into the 1989 campaign, Doug, his driver, the state trooper and I made a stop in Grundy. It's that part of Virginia's isolated panhandle that, culturally, is more Tennessee and Kentucky than Virginia. It's a conservative bedrock, proud of its Southern heritage, where houses, pick-ups and even businesses proudly fly the Stars and Bars flag. We pulled up to a small restaurant with such a display. The guys were hungry and wanted to get some food, but I paused.

"I ain't going in there, because we may not walk out. Those rednecks will shoot us deader than a hammer," I told Doug, who was, as usual, riding in the front seat. Doug laughed. "If you don't come I'll leave you here ... Don't worry, I know these people. We'll be fine," he said. A teenage boy took our order.

I asked for a glass of fresh-squeezed orange juice. The young waiter snapped, "We don't squeeze no oranges 'round here." Doug leaned into the boy and admonished, "Well, son, you're gonna squeeze some today." I got my orange juice, but didn't touch it. As we were leaving, Doug said, "We went through all of that and you're not even gonna drink it?" I said, "Doug, there's probably something in that glass that looks like orange juice but isn't."

Later that day, I watched Doug work an audience of several hundred Grundy supporters cheering his name, waving his campaign placards and American flags. The faces were black and white. What I feared would turn into an embarrassing blunder became another success. That happened a lot with Doug. He did, indeed, know these people and the mood in Virginia.

We won the election by the narrowest margin, less than one-half of a percentage point. And we survived a recount. As a black governor from a Southern state, Doug Wilder became a national political force overnight. He was on TV talk shows and newscasts as a symbol of the gains black Americans had made. He was also seen as a middle-of-the-road Democrat, a fiscal conservative with a heart.

Governor Wilder appointed me to a couple of state boards, including the University of Virginia's. I attended lots of dinners in the governor's mansion and was a fly-on-the-wall at many high-level meetings. Doug and I talked regularly, sometimes several times a day. The media portrayed me as the governor's closest confidant. Doug never denied that and later said, "Everyone needs someone to talk to."

Through Doug, I began to understand the force and faults of politics. Nearly every politician I had come to know, including Doug, was fueled by idealism and good intentions. The idea that those who enter politics are evil or inherently corrupt is nonsense. I suppose there are people in office who become corrupt, and there are certainly lots who make bad choices, but I never saw lying, cheating or stealing or even suspected it.

What I did see was Doug and others wrestle with compromise. I remember often thinking that I wouldn't want to be confronted with such tough, gut-wrenching choices. More than once, I was in the executive mansion when an eleventh-hour call came in from a prison inmate facing execution. These were truly life-or-death choices that often pitted personal beliefs against political necessity. More than a dozen executions occurred on Doug's watch. I remember thinking that it's easy to forgive a murderer if you don't have to look the victim's family members in the eyes, and it's easy to say "kill the bastard" if you're not the one giving the order.

Doug and I talked about the consequences of such decisions and about lots of other personal stuff. Doug was a trial lawyer by training and could dissect an issue, carefully weighing its merits and making certain he had the pertinent facts. Doug didn't rush to action or allow himself to be bullied. When he made a decision, he was decisive and rarely apologetic. Once his mind was made up, he would confidently move on.

Through him, I realized elected office might not be in the cards for me. We discussed me entering the political fray, and I had even been asked several times to consider making a run for statewide office. I could give a speech and certainly knew how to lead and motivate others. But it was becoming clear to me that the price of holding political office was steep and potentially damaging. Another problem: It's hard to get elected when you're a political Independent.

I watched the media and critics ravage Chuck Robb. This was a former Marine, who, as governor, was considered boring because he was so ramrod straight and clean-cut. Suddenly he was being crucified as a deviant. Chuck survived the Beach party scandal, but by 1991 was being pummeled again over allegations that, while governor, he had an eighteen-month affair with a former Miss Virginia. The haranguing witch hunt never seemed to stop. At about the same time, some two and a half years after the fact, the tape recording of my conversation with Doug surfaced. The tape was leaked to the Robb camp and then to the press—mostly as an effort to embarrass Doug, I believe. Three of Chuck's staffers resigned as result of the scandal and criminal charges were brought.

Chuck further embarrassed himself and his family when he admitted that he had received a nude massage from that former beauty queen, Tai Collins, in a New York hotel, but did not have sex with her. The entire mess was pathetic. Too many high-profile leaders were public targets, not just public servants. I had no interest in living life with a bull's-eye on my back. I just didn't have the stomach for it. The transparency of politics made me appreciate my privacy and the seclusion of Point Farm even more.

I had lived pretty wildly and freely, at least by the puritanical standards of some. I traveled a lot, entertained a lot and was around many young, attractive women. I made no apologies for having a good time, and I didn't want to be in a position of having to explain myself to anyone. I figured that if a straight-arrow like Chuck Robb could get flogged by the press and political enemies for attending a few parties and getting a massage, I'd get burned at the stake. I was an ethical businessman who hustled to grow a company and who shared my largesse with others by taking people on trips, buying them gifts and picking up the tab for countless dinners and parties. Frankly, I found the country club set stuffy and boring.

I wasn't, by any means, ordained or a saint, which appeared to be the new standards for holding high political office. I would never want to subject my two young daughters and two little boys to tawdry gossip. No, my private life would remain private, and personal conversations would remain such. I would live vicariously through those with the courage and conviction to brave public office, and I would put my energy and resources behind those I most admired.

Doug had become a regular at the Farm, mostly just to have a place to relax and escape the limelight of public life. But even at the Shore, having him there was also a bit of a sideshow. When he arrived by land it was usually with an escort, and he often shuttled between the state capital and the Farm by helicopter. He had become somewhat of a regular. He once landed so close to the house that the draft from the copter blades filled the pool with leaves. Doug was nice enough to try and scoop some out.

Lots of introductions were made at the Farm. Through Doug I met future governor and now U.S. Senator Mark Warner, the cell phone millionaire and Harvard law graduate who loved politics and ran Wilder's campaign. Mark would be my best man at my third wedding years later. I also became very close to Dr. William R. Harvey, president of Hampton University. Bill and I had worked together on Doug's campaign finance committee. Like Doug, he was raised in the segregated South and was deeply motivated by his parents to succeed professionally and help others of his race. We became good friends and forged a business relationship that has lasted two decades.

As my circle of influence and friendships expanded, so did the calls from those wanting political favors. For many, particularly strangers, I politely listened to their requests and simply did nothing. However, I would, when invited, recommend to the governor or his staff names of those who I thought might be a good candidate for a political appointment or even judgeship. And there were several. I respected the governor and our relationship by only endorsing someone for a board or office whose abilities or motivations were not in doubt. You don't get many political chits with governors or any high-level elected officials. So you had better use the chits you do have wisely. And you never want to embarrass friends in high places with bad advice or dumb comments that can circle back.

People think that I have had more influence to affect policy and decisions than I really have. I've been an advisor and made my position on an issue known more than once. But the fact is, once in office, politicians and their decisions are closely scrutinized by their staffs, by legal watchdogs, the media and their foes. I have never asked a governor for anything for me or my company. The assumption is that government is one huge good ol' boys' network of cronyism and favors. It's more like a hundred little networks, many of which are vying for the same things.

Decades ago, there was a lot more unabashed glad-handing. But disclosure and bidding laws enforced by watchdog agencies now make it very difficult and very risky to seek or accept favoritism. In fact, having close political ties can become a liability because of perceptions of favoritism.

In 1993, some political foes of Doug's started sniffing around for a scandal after my company won an open bid contract to renovate an old state office building in Richmond. The state bought the Main Street property in 1990 without realizing it was loaded with asbestos. Times were lean for my company so we applied to be one of the bidders to renovate and modernize the old hulk. At first, state officials didn't even allow Armada Hoffler on the list of qualified contractors, claiming we had a couple of bad references. We appealed and provided a long list of positive references on several big jobs we had completed, a list that dwarfed the couple of complaints from naysayers. As a result of our appeal, we were allowed to bid and ultimately beat out a half-dozen other firms with low bids of less than sixteen million. Even that turned into a controversy, with some saying we had inside information. That was totally ridiculous. We received the same bid specs at the same time as everyone else.

We won the job but the renovation turned into a nightmare. Our workers started finding dangerous amounts of asbestos in areas of the building that were supposed to have been without any. The state had asked us to modify the original plans, which would mean knocking out some walls. But those officials never provided diagrams showing us locations for pockets of asbestos. The deeper we got into the job the more of a mess we discovered. It took us longer, and it cost more money than expected, to make the building safe.

The cost overruns provoked an investigation and sparked allegations in the Richmond newspaper that the governor or his cronies had steered the job to me and my company and the state was now overpaying. That was complete nonsense. I never spoke to Doug about the Main Street project. I was so infuriated that I held a press conference at a Richmond hotel and asked for a full inquiry by the state to get the facts out. The governor did the same. An investigation by a state Senate subcommittee concluded that the architect hired by the state to design the asbestos removal plan never coordinated with the architects designing the renovation. Our construction guys were caught in the middle. The governor ultimately blasted those in charge for incompetence that tacked an extra four million to the price of the project. The witch hunt ended favorably for Armada Hoffler and me; we had done nothing wrong. But the fiasco had caused us a lot of grief and called into question the governor's integrity and mine.

For me, about the only substantive payoff from having political connections is making even more political connections and seeing how decisions are made. But once you join that political herd, you're fair game. One of the great advantages of being plugged in politically is being tapped to sit as a director on a prestigious board. You get to see these extremely bright and talented leaders in action, dealing with complex issues at a table filled with other big personalities and egos. You can quickly get a handle on how people, those who are difficult or obnoxious, quickly show their tendencies during tough decisions. More skilled leaders stake out common ground in a debate, looking to build consensus around areas of agreement.

I learned a lot by keeping my mouth shut and observing different leadership styles. Being personable, respectful of others and maintaining a sense of humor can be as potent as being technically savvy and "right." Know what you know and don't be too proud to admit what you don't. Ask questions, but don't argue. The same is true in private life.

My business relationships with people almost always started out personal. I'd meet them over dinner or at a party or fundraiser; we would discover we both had hunted, or fished, or like traveling to the same places or had a mutual friend. I'd invite them to the Farm to shoot or for dinner or to horseback ride. I'd eventually introduce them to others who I thought they'd enjoy meeting, and they'd do the same for me.

Building this web was a gradual process that spread randomly, like tree roots. There was no master plan or checklist. You can't necessarily connect dots from one relationship to another or from one business deal to the next. It's more organic, what I call a slow, steady burn. Over time, the who-you-know web takes on a life of its own. In some ways it's like being the popular kid in school; the more friends you have, the more you make. I don't think people ever really change in that way.

I can tell you that networking is not only good for business, it is business. Anyone saying otherwise is either lying, in denial or naïve. Business is personal. When you're doing multimillion-dollar deals with someone, you had better like them or at least know them well enough to trust them. That's especially true when times are tough. If not for the strong relationships we had with a few lenders, especially a couple guys at the Bank of America, Armada Hoffler would have been significantly more bruised by the 1990 recession. Our lenders stuck with us, and we didn't want to let them down. Even when we were losing money on a deal or struggling to cover our debt service, we made damn certain to keep our loan officers informed. We did restructure a few loans and sell off assets, but we never defaulted.

Instead of whining about the economy, we used the dog days of the early 1990s to reposition the company for the recovery, which, we all knew, would come. Relationship building at Point Farm had helped set the table for our next growth spurt.

CHAPTER XII
Rebound

"You can't deal with the way things were.
You have to deal with the way things are."

I was worried about the futures of executives and many loyal employees who had been in our development, real estate and property management divisions. Frankly, things were slow and we were having a hard time making the numbers for those divisions. By 1991, we had to lay off nearly a third of our workforce and were struggling to keep the one hundred and eighty or so remaining workers busy. Our construction division kept the money rolling in by seguing into government work.

Throughout most of the 1980s, we generally avoided the extremely competitive world of bidding on building contracts for schools, courthouses and other municipal projects. It's a cutthroat business that forces contractors to cut corners. Generally, those who can do a job the cheapest get the contract.

Profit margins are so slim that contractors can lose money if they don't bid a job exactly right, or if material costs unexpectedly increase. When you're working for nickels, everyone feels the pinch, even the carpenters, electricians and other hardhat tradesmen hired to actually build a project. General contractors, those awarded the job, have to beat down their subcontractors on cost to make the numbers work. That creates tension and indifference.

Lou Haddad and his team were very good at getting costs down on the front end. A lot of competitors saved four or five percent through cutthroat negotiations with their subs or material suppliers. If companies simply hired us, instead of awarding work through open bidding, our guys could shave ten percent off the price by working with a company's architects and engineers during the design phase. Architects like to jazz buildings up with fancy angels and materials. Sometimes that required customized steel beams or glass that had to be fabricated. Special ordering that stuff takes a lot of time, and it's expensive. Our guys saved big by using off-the-shelf materials that were immediately available. Lou likes to say that when we start a job we have everything we need stacked in the parking lot.

We didn't make much money on municipal work and sometimes it could be a pain. If you mess up, critics publicly condemn you. That happened once when we built a city jail. The project had some design flaws and city engineers kept making changes. That increased costs and delayed the work, setting off alarms among some city and media watchdogs. The scrutiny became so bad that the FBI was called in to investigate. We really had no idea what exactly was being investigated. We assumed there must have been some pretty serious allegations tied to how jail construction funds were being spent. We were overbudget and the project planning had not gone well, but we kept very meticulous records and accounted for all expenses, as we do on all of our jobs.

I always believe in getting in front of a problem and being forthright. I called Lou Haddad into the office and told him to immediately meet with local FBI agents to answer any questions and to make it clear we would make every stitch of paperwork on the project available. We did just that. We brought boxes and boxes of files into a conference room and neatly organized them for the agents. There were literally thousands of pages.

We didn't hear anything for months from the FBI or the city. Finally, we received word that there would be no case or charges, but we were never told exactly what had been investigated or what we supposedly did wrong. We completed the job and wound up dividing some of the cost overruns with the city. We barely covered our expenses on that deal, which, of course, didn't get reported by the local media. We learned some very valuable lessons from that experience: When working on projects involving taxpayer money, you need to be beyond reproach. Everything is an open book.

Thankfully, most of our government jobs went smoothly, which enabled us to keep our network of subcontractors and Armada Hoffler managers on the payroll. We had a stellar track record of successes and a long list of very satisfied customers. When you step up to the plate as many times as our company had, you're bound to hit a few foul balls. I doubt there is a company anywhere that bats one thousand.

It took us nearly a decade to build an impressive workforce at Armada Hoffler and we didn't want to lose it, so during the tough times we sucked it up and took the best jobs we could find—even if it was government work. That turned out to be a very fortuitous decision.

The city of Norfolk had for years been trying to establish

itself as a regional destination for business and conventions. It had a couple of public facilities, but they were dated and small. The city also lacked enough decent hotel space. The two go hand in hand. If you want to host big conventions, you need enough rooms to accommodate guests.

Building hotels had been risky business and banks had long lost their appetite to back such deals. Richard M. Stormont, for one, had figured out another way to get big projects built. Dick had been a senior executive with Marriott for years. He was an extremely smart guy, holding an M.B.A. from Cornell in hospitality management. Dick left Marriott in 1984 and started his own firm, basing it in Atlanta. His timing was perfect. Lots of landmark hotels around the country were dated and needed replacing. At the same time, new commercial centers were sprouting, competing with older ones, like Norfolk, which were fighting to stay alive.

Dick knew that cities had some interesting ways to raise money for public projects that didn't involve banks. A city could raise cash by hiking taxes, of course, or it could issue bonds that would be bought by investors. Those bonds were like gold, a pretty safe investment. It was like taxpayers cosigning a loan. The revenue from bond sales had been used to pay for lots of big municipal projects, things like new sewers, parking garages, airports and industrial parks. Dick Stormont figured cities could take the same approach with hotels and convention centers. The bonds could be paid off over time with profits from those projects. And, if the formula worked, other shops and restaurants around the big hotel would feed off of the tourists like pilot fish on sharks, making more money and rewarding the city with more tax revenue. Hotels and convention centers would be incubators.

Norfolk was anxious not to get left behind neighboring Virginia Beach and coastal cities to the south feeding on conventioneers, so it partnered with Dick to build a twenty-three floor Marriott hotel with four hundred and five rooms. The city would own and operate a four-floor convention center with two large ballrooms connected to the hotel tower.

Dick was aware of Armada Hoffler and had met Lou. At one point, he even approached us about doing some of the work on the Norfolk project. At the time, we hadn't built anything over six stories. We had the expertise but nothing in our construction portfolio to prove we could handle a high-rise project on our own. We politely declined to participate.

A construction company working with Dick had been drafting plans for the Norfolk Waterside Marriott and Waterside Convention Center. The cost projections came in way high, creating a panic and almost scuttling the deal. Dick dumped his own team and prodded us to consider taking the lead on construction. We were nervous, but confident. We had several staffers who had done high-rise buildings with previous employers, and we knew how to keep expenses down by working with building designers. We would apply the same approach but on a much larger scale, actually a scale three-to-four times larger than anything we had done.

When it was announced that Armada Hoffler was chosen to build the fifty-two-million-dollar project, Norfolk's local paper said it was like asking a plumber to do brain surgery. Our critics were suddenly mute when we finished the job ahead of schedule and within budget. We even received a performance bonus and held our annual company Christmas party at the hotel. The complex opened in November 1991, cementing our reputation. Almost instantly, we went from being a "local" company to a big-time hotel builder. All of a sudden, we became the "big deal guys, the high-rise guys," Lou would say.

Dick went on to do nearly twenty public-private hotel and

convention centers, and we built several, including a seven-hundred-room Marriott in Baltimore and the two-hundred-and-fifty-room Renaissance Portsmouth Hotel and Waterfront Conference Center on the waterfront in Portsmouth. The Stormont deals led to others and in years to come would graduate to marquee projects like the Mandarin Oriental Hotel in Washington, and the Four Seasons and Marriott hotel towers in Baltimore.

Construction work definitely carried the company through the recession, which had lingered in Hampton Roads. Other cities, and even northern Virginia, were getting back on track, but we continued to drag locally, mostly because of cuts in defense spending. We felt the pain in our real estate development arm, and to a lesser, but nonetheless alarming extent, our property management division. They were in trouble.

We hadn't built a single project owned or operated by Armada Hoffler in nearly four years. The rents had plummeted and vacancy rates had increased on several of the properties we were managing. We had a lot of very talented but very expensive managers and agents on our staff without enough to do. They weren't bringing in much money, which had become a drag on our finances.

That wasn't unique to Armada Hoffler. Commercial real estate firms all over were treading water or drowning in the recession. Some merged to stay afloat, others disappeared. We had heard that one of the biggest, most prestigious firms in the state was among those gasping—Norfolk-based Goodman Segar Hogan.

Goodman Segar Hogan's commercial real estate division had been bought in the late 1980s by Dominion Resources, the Richmond, Virginia, Fortune 500 that owns Virginia Power, the state's behemoth electric utility. Dominion owned several large tracts in the state and elsewhere and bought Goodman Segar Hogan during the 1980s boom to help develop and manage its properties.

A couple of our guys knew some of the key players at Goodman Segar Hogan and the person with Dominion who controlled the firm. We thought we might be able to turn two losers into a winner by marrying our development and management businesses. The idea was at least worth a shot.

Goodman Segar Hogan was an old money firm that had deep ties with some banks and various other movers and shakers around the state. The company name crowned the crescent-shaped, glass façade office building overlooking the Elizabeth River. For years, the building had been the marquee office in downtown Norfolk and arguably the region. It had its own lunch and dinner club—the area's premier business venue—conference rooms and a collection of well-heeled firms leasing office space. The building had an Old South country club feel and was just down the road from Norfolk's yacht club and two blocks from the Marriott we had just built.

In our view, Goodman Segar Hogan had grown tired and flabby living off its laurels. It still had a great reputation on the outside, but its finances were a mess. It had too much overhead and some of its business practices were dated. If we could merge our culture with their name, we might have a winner.

In June 1993, we did just that. We kicked around a new name for a few months and agreed on Goodman Segar Hogan Hoffler. Dominion retained a majority share but our crew took over management. Russ negotiated the deal and pretty much shaped the financial game plan. Neither side put in cash. Rather, we grafted our expertise onto the Goodman Segar Hogan name and combined our portfolios of property under management. Russ and I swiftly moved several of our very best real estate and finance experts to run the new independent firm, including Rick Burnell, who had been with me from the start.

I had a lot of personal satisfaction the day the new sign was placed on Norfolk's World Trade Center. I heard through the grapevine that some of the old guard cringed. I had merged my way into their circle and now owned the lunch and dinner club where they broke bread.

Russ, Rick and the crew wasted no time. Within the first few months we cut more than one million dollars in overhead. We blended the staffs, provided much firmer financial guidelines and consolidated property management operations. As one company, we had instantly doubled the portfolio of property managed or owned and ran it with far fewer people. Within a year, we were making money.

One of the best windfalls in that deal for me was befriending Thomas Capps, the top guy at Dominion Resources. Tom was a lawyer by training, and a career utility man, well-respected for his technical and management savvy. He was understated, usually to the point, but witty and elegant. Tom was an avid wing shooter and frequent guest at the Farm. We traveled to Europe several times to hunt grouse in Scotland and Spain. These were more gentlemanly outings with guides and game drivers, world-class chefs and sommeliers. These trips reminded me how far from Portsmouth, Virginia, I had come. This was a long way from putting chicken parts on a hook and fishing for carp or sunfish.

Tom took me under his wing and became a very close friend and mentor. He often traveled with his business entourage, giving me a chance to see how he interacted with and delegated to his top people. Tom was also extremely politically savvy and had been repeatedly tapped to sit on several private and public boards, including the College of William & Mary.

Tom and his people at Dominion were impressed with Goodman Segar Hogan Hoffler's results and decided to double down on their bet. We absorbed two Richmond real estate companies and another in Washington, basically using the same merger formula. We later scooped up a firm in Raleigh. Within just a few years, Goodman Segar Hogan Hoffler had more than two hundred employees and was managing more than a billion dollars' worth of office and industrial space. That number would swell to five billion. When we sold the firm in 1998, Dominion and Armada Hoffler made seventeen million dollars. It was a textbook acquisition, merger and sale.

Around the same period, we hit another homerun without even stepping up to the plate. We were in the process of buying about an acre of land in Washington Harbour in Georgetown. We were planning an office complex and in the final stages of signing tenants and finalizing the deal. Crescent Real Estate Equity, a Dallas-based conglomerate, had just purchased a complex next to our lot and wanted the patch of ground to protect its investment preserve open space. Crescent bought our contract from us and in less than three months paid us what would have been our profit had we done the project—eight million dollars. It was another textbook deal, one that got even better. About five years later, we bought back the same parcel and used it to build the Swedish Embassy and an adjacent office-and-condo complex. We made eight figures on that deal, a stunning profit. That parcel turned into a nexus of opportunity and perfect timing.

The other piston driving our growth had been a rapidly expanding college across the James River. Hampton University was emerging as one of the elite historically black schools in the country. The school was run by Bill Harvey, my former colleague on Wilder's campaign. Bill is an extremely smart guy with the rare blend of business savvy and high-academic achievement.

He earned a doctorate degree from Harvard and in 1986 became the first African American to own a Pepsi Bottling Co. franchise.

Bill served with me on Doug's finance committee and helped raise and managed a lot of money for the campaign. As with me, Bill came from fairly modest means and had tremendous role models. His father was a Civil Rights leader in segregated Alabama and prospered by launching his own construction business. Bill's mom drilled fiscal prudence into her son, teaching him to buy only what he could afford to pay for at the time. Bill understood, fundamentally, that success springs from hard work and a relentless focus on opportunity, not obstacles. He also had a fixed moral compass that formed during his younger years as a highly decorated Boy Scout. He was, and is, a man of his word. "I was taught by my parents that your word is your bond," Bill says.

He was named head of Hampton University about a year before I launched Armada Hoffler. When we met, we both had the wind at our backs and a lot we wanted to accomplish. We were both self-made and on a trajectory of growth. "It was like we were brothers in the universe," Bill says. Competitive brothers. Bill was playing a lot of tennis, as was I. So I invited him to Point Farm for a match. He whopped me, and I haven't played him since. Bill occasionally reminds me of that ill-fated showdown when I start bragging about my golf game or athleticism.

Bill's goal was to transform Hampton University into one of the preeminent destinations for African-American students. To make that happen, he would have to build an aesthetically attractive campus with state of the art facilities. And, to do that, he needed lots of money.

Bill grew the school with the verve of a company CEO. He would leave his social imprint on the school by embracing the business side of running a large institution instead of viewing it as a necessary evil of the academic world. Through the school he would build and operate shopping centers and apartment complexes for the students, putting profits back into the campus.

I remember some of my earliest meetings with Bill. I quickly learned,personally and professionally, that he did what he said he would do and was always reasonable and collaborative. He laid out the vision for his school and we would, building by building, help make that happen. "In our society, there are a lot of people who tell you what you want to hear," Bill says. "Dan and his company were always honest and did what they said they would do." My company and I always shot straight with Bill and the university. We gave him our best price, never cut corners and if we ran into a problem, we worked on a solution together.

Just as in the movie "Field of Dreams," Bill Harvey built it and they came. The student population over the years has tripled as Bill spent close to fifty million on eighteen new buildings and renovations. Armada Hoffler did pretty much all of that construction.

CHAPTER XIII
Tradeoffs

*"You don't go through this journey and come out
without scars. It's the other side of being blessed."*

The go-go 1990s had been great for business and for me,
personally. It was fun to be around success and others who
enjoyed it too. Melissa and I had become friends with or close
acquaintances of celebrities, professional athletes and big
names in business and the military: novelist Patricia Cornwell,
Atlanta Braves Manager Bobby Cox, sausage king Jimmy Dean,
Chief of Naval Operations Jay Johnson, to name a few. All were
fascinating to listen to at the dinner table or over drinks, and
there were many things to learn from each. These folks were at
the top of their games, and it was fascinating hearing how they
got there and how they handled it. One of my closest and most
enduring friendships would be with a young man from Norfolk
who did his job better than anyone.

I met Bruce Smith at a political fundraiser in 1993 when he was in his eighth season as a defensive end and on his way to the NFL's Hall of Fame as the league's all-time quarterback sack leader. Bruce's shoulders were as wide and steely as the grill on a Mack truck, and his legs had the speed of a Ferrari. You didn't have to be an NFL fan to

NFL Hall of Fame inductee Bruce Smith and I

appreciate Bruce's formidable athleticism. The man clearly had the brawn, but he also had a fast mind and unrelenting work ethic that kept him healthy and fit throughout his career. Professional football is as much about longevity as prowess, and Bruce had both.

Bruce was six foot three, two hundred and sixty pounds when he graduated high school in Norfolk, and he wasn't done growing. He went on to become a football icon at Virginia Tech, smashing school records, offensive linemen and quarterbacks. He was the top pick in the NFL draft and already considered one the most gifted athletes in Virginia history.

Bruce spent most of his nineteen years in the NFL with the Buffalo Bills before finishing out his storied career closer to home with the Washington Redskins. It was there where he got his two hundredth quarterback sack, an NFL record.

Bruce started thinking early about life after the NFL. He could have lived a life on golf courses and beaches after retiring, making money signing autographs and doing appearances. He was a megastar with lots of money and hordes of admirers.

I liked Bruce as soon as we met. He was affable, down-to-earth and clearly a very bright guy. Like most in Virginia, I already knew his story: He grew up in Norfolk and attended an urban high school, Booker T. Washington. His family was humble and hardworking. His mom worked in a plastic factory and raised the three children. His dad was, as Bruce put it, "God fearing" and instilled his kids with a strong work ethic. When we met, I could see this wasn't just urban legend. This young man had character.

Bruce almost didn't play football. He quit the high school team after his second practice because football was "too hot, too hard and too painful." Bruce decided to, instead, stick with basketball. The football coach called looking for Bruce and wound up speaking to his dad. Not too long afterward, Bruce's dad asked his son why he skipped practice. When Bruce gave his reason, his father admonished him never to give up, a lesson Bruce embraced throughout his career.

I wanted to get to know Bruce, so I invited him to Point Farm. Bruce accepted and over the next two years we built a close friendship and enjoyed lots of laughs. "I liked the fact that Dan wasn't stuck-up," Bruce says. "He wasn't one of those people." I felt the same way about him. I'd like to pretend that I was as much of an athlete as Bruce and would ask him to get me in at least one NFL play, "just one play" to prove myself. "Dan thinks he's a real comedian," Bruce says.

Bruce became increasingly interested in commercial real estate, and just as with professional football, he became a student of this other sport. Bruce saw that many of the attributes needed to excel on the gridiron were at play in the business world. He clearly wasn't interested in being a passive investor, no more than he would have been interested in sitting on the bench in the NFL. Bruce wanted to know about the guts of a business deal, how it's structured, the various risks, the math behind calculating returns on investment, the details of financing. "I wanted to understand the deal; I wanted to understand the process," Bruce says.

After a couple of years getting to know Bruce, he partnered

with my company on a project in Florida. He picked the right one, because it turned out to be a very successful venture. That became one of the first of many business deals Bruce entered into with me and the company. He continues to work very closely with Armada Hoffler and remains a confidant, companion and frequent guest.

In the mid-1990s, entertaining at the Farm and traveling to pursue a business deal or to hunt absorbed most of my time. Plus, I had four kids in various stages of life. Sara was off to college; Kristy was finishing high school; the boys, Daniel and Hunter, liked spending quality time with me. Melissa was running the farm, setting our social agenda, raising the kids, doing volunteer work and trying to stay involved with her passion for horse eventing.

Our lives were packed with family, friends and dinner parties. All seemed busy, hectic but good. Despite the many stresses of time management, Melissa and I got along great and we never traded a cross word. But in hindsight, I don't think we spent enough time alone, just walking or talking or simply enjoying each other's company. We were always doing fun stuff, just not a lot of it together.

Our network of close friends was shocked and saddened to learn that Melissa and I were divorcing. The details of what triggered this decision were very painful. Our marriage blew up and, after a year of legal wrangling,was dissolved. Usually, my holidays are filled with parties and people. The New Year's Eve after the breakup, it was just me and my youngest daughter, Kristy. My young sons were living in a new home with their mother and my oldest daughter was with her college sweetheart.

Despite the emotional bruising, I have to give Melissa credit for being a good mother to our sons and encouraging my ongoing and close relationship with our boys. Although they lived with her most of the time, my sons spent much of their summers and long stretches of holidays with me. Melissa and I collaborated on raising our boys; they have turned out to be great young men. All four of my kids are respectful and have great personalities. I have always thought that if I can raise them the way my parents raised me, I will have been a success.

Just as in my childhood home, my kids were not yelled or cursed at or harshly punished. They have all done things that I disagree with or that I have found upsetting. Before letting my emotions fly, I always thought carefully about what I wanted to say—and where to say it. Sometimes I ambushed them by raising an issue at dinner; sometimes I'd summon them into my office at home or have them come to work. A car ride with me was the most-feared venue because there was no escape. I always tried to make my kids understand the consequences of their behavior: If they were to get into trouble it embarrasses not only them, but our family. That kind of outside scrutiny comes with the territory of having wealth and a public name. I cautioned them about the company they kept and the motivations of those around them. I did not want my kids to grow up untrusting or cynical, but I did want them to be cautious. They needed to understand the value of giving and receiving loyalty.

I don't think any of my kids would say that they ever feared me, but I am pretty certain all four would agree that they do not want to disappoint me. And I'm pretty sure each of them likes hanging out with each other and their dad. We joke and tease each other, and I have always encouraged them to bring friends around. Most parents love their children, as do I. But I also like my kids. Each has a great personality and warm heart. As children, my kids were always respectful of adults without prompting, addressing them as "sir" and "ma'am."

As far as their own occupations, I have not pressured any of them to be my heir apparent in business or to pursue any particular profession or job. Sure, I want them to be financially successful, but most important is finding a path that excites them. Kristy lived in New York after college and flirted with going into show business. Sara helped run a nonprofit. Did I help them? You bet. I've done the same for my sons and will for my grandkids. I have tried to do enough for my offspring so that they can do something fulfilling with their lives, but I have avoided giving them too much. I don't want to rob them of the drive to make their own personal marks on the world.

Very successful people often have lots of demands on their time and that sometimes means that those closest get neglected. It's common among people of celebrity and wealth. I have, at times, been a neglectful husband, but I have tried to always be an attentive dad, just as my parents were attentive to me.

My personal life has been in sharp contrast to my mother and father's relationship, however. Nearly every aspect of their lives has been intertwined. Alfred ate dinner at home nearly every night and when they traveled or went out for the night, they did so together. They remained constant companions because they loved each other and because they felt secure together. They needed each other emotionally and financially. I have had the means to move on when a relationship crashed on the rocks.

Alfred and Sarah never admonished me for my failed marriages or disparaged my ex-wives or other women in my life. They were sad that these relationships had failed, and they felt bad for my children. Instead of finger pointing, they supported me and did all they could to remain attentive and loving to my children. They knew my world was different and in many ways far more complex. They did as they always had: They tried to understand instead of judge.

When you have a lot of success or money you become less dependent on others. The world becomes a supermarket—you pick and choose what you want and move on to the next aisle.

You simply don't have to stay in a bad relationship or marriage for financial reasons, and I never would just for appearances. I have seen many miserable people stay married because they wanted to avoid the embarrassment of divorce.

One thing is pretty much the same for everyone, rich or poor—you get a much better sense of who your friends really are when you're going through a rough patch. Some people are quick to choose sides and cast stones. Others pretend to be empathetic. In my divorces, I lost a few friends who condemned me. The same happened to my ex-wives. Everyone loses something in a divorce and among those hit hardest were some close friends and family who cared about both sides. I don't wish that kind of loss or pain on anyone.

The best way to rebound from significant setbacks is to quickly move away from them and get on with life. I have found that those who live in the past are generally depressed. When people wallow in self-pity, flog themselves or avoid change, they become stagnant, which triggers a cycle of even more despair. I have seen it hundreds of times, and frankly, I don't understand it. I've always looked for the lessons in mistakes and eventually muster enough self-confidence to laugh at my own gaffes and recognize my flaws. I remember my lawyer kidding me that he was probably the only divorce attorney in Virginia kept on retainer. That stung when he said it, but it rang true. I knew I'd be fine because I could laugh at his joke.

I dated several great women between marriages and even had a long-term relationship with one who I lived with for a while. Each brought me joy and helped me move on. This sounds cliché, but life is short. I don't know what happens after people die, other than the fact that we're dead for a long time; so I have always tried to stay positive, enjoy myself and lean on those who I trust most.

My partners at Armada Hoffler had kept the business stable

through the rough times, and as we emerged from the recession, our bottom line improved. I also had a core of loyal friends who I still enjoyed spending time with, and my passion for hunting and the outdoors remained stoked.

I pursued my zeal for bird hunting and fishing on three continents. I made an annual tradition of taking a few friends with me to pheasant hunt in South Dakota or to hunt ducks and dove in Argentina. One of my most adventurous and remote trips had been piranha fishing with a couple of friends in the Amazon. It was hot, bug infested and eye-opening. Hunting or fishing trips often lead to remote and very impoverished parts of the world. Indigenous people often live, literally, on dirt or in huts if they're lucky. Sometimes they're so desperate for money they'll do the unconscionable. On my Amazon adventure, a father in a village offered his young son for sex. It was a sickening and sad moment, one no doubt born out of desperation. In Argentina, I saw children running barefoot and naked along riverbanks and living a few feet away under a blue tarp tied to tree branches. Often, these stories were more compelling than the hunt itself, but they're seldom told. This was the raw side of the world that doesn't show up in glossy hunting brochures or in travel guides.

William "Buddy" Bethea, my personal doctor and friend, coaxed me into joining him on a trip he promised would be uplifting and a challenge—a moose hunt in Alaska. I had been on a few more gentlemanly estate deer hunts in Scotland and, of course, shot whitetail on the Eastern Shore. But this would be my first real big game quest.

Alaska was as advertised—beautiful and remote. We went in August when the land, at least at lower altitudes, was dry. Riding into our base camp on horseback added to the adventure. We ate jerky, had coffee in the cool mornings, waded barefoot through streams to keep our boots dry and hiked until our backs ached. The temperatures bounced each day from cold to warm to cold. The purity of the place and its air was as invigorating as the landscape. I loved the seclusion and the physical test of hunting and tracking in rugged terrain. Suddenly, I had big game fever and a new passion.

One of the most prestigious quests in the hunting world is called the big horn sheep "Grand Slam." I had read about these great creatures, rams that live on the vertical terrain in North American mountains. A male can weigh three hundred pounds and have massive curled horns that weigh thirty. They move in small groups or solo, often living at more than seven thousand feet and traveling narrow trails that hug cliffs and weave through peaks and valleys.

Achieving a Grand Slam takes a lot of money and time. The animal populations are carefully controlled and permits to pursue one can cost several thousand dollars each. Buying the right equipment isn't cheap, and neither is hiring a professional guide. Without one, you don't stand much of a chance of even seeing a bighorn let alone getting within rifle shot distance.

Me sleeping in a cave during a bighorn sheep hunt in 2001

Four types of bighorn sheep make up the Grand Slam: the Dall, Stone, Rocky Mountain and Desert. Their range extends along a spine of mountains extending from Alaska onward south to Mexico. You don't just grab a rifle and go. These trips are physically demanding endurance tests, and the weather can be extreme. Hunters need to be in what guides call "sheep" shape. The hunts can be a two-week grind of walking up and down trails no wider than your arm span or over loose rocks. You trek in the rain, sleet and snow, hope that the mountain fog clears, and when the day is done, you sleep in a tent, under the stars, or if you're lucky enough, a cave.

I worked out six months to prep my legs, back and lungs for the ordeal, which would involve five trips spread over three years. First on my list was the Stone sheep in the Yukon Territory, then the Dall in Brooks Range, Alaska, then the Desert bighorn in Hermosillo, Mexico, and finally, the Rocky Mountain bighorn in British Columbia, the rarest and most challenging.

I was in pretty good shape to begin with, but even so, there aren't many guys fifty or older who take on such a grueling challenge. For me, that was part of the appeal. Not only do you need endurance, but you'd better have decent balance as well. Mountain trails can be uneven and slippery. There are rocks to step over and around on nearly every angle imaginable and you're traversing with a thirty-pound backpack and a rifle. The guide carries even more weight, including most of the food and tents.

Many of the days begin and end the same. You rise early, have as much breakfast as you can hold, break camp and then start hunting. One of the first stops is a lookout point where you "glass" the mountain peaks in the distance and valleys below for sheep through binoculars or a rifle scope. It takes several hours some days for the sun to burn off mountain fog, so you mostly sit and wait or traverse slowly. Once animals are spotted, the guide's job is to get you in close enough for a shot. But that's easier said than done. The sheep don't stay in one place for long and are extremely wary. They have great eyesight and smell. One whiff of you and they scamper up or down a ledge and out of sight.

Some days we'd walk for ten hours, taking off our shoes when we crossed a stream or creek, stopping only to get our bearings or glass the horizon. It's extremely important to have clothes and boots that ventilate well and dry quickly. When you're traveling up and down, you're constantly moving into different weather zones. Some days it would be raining below and snowing on top. Or there might be a fog bowl on one side of the mountain face and full sun on the other. The cold and wet and shifting temperatures grind you down. Some days I'd be too exhausted to eat. I just wanted to crawl inside my sleeping bag. Each sheep hunt I took melted five to ten pounds off me and left me with a roadmap of sprains, bruises and dried cracked skin. But I also came away with a bank full of memories from some of the most beautiful landscapes in the world—and some fabulous trophies. I became the nine hundred and sixty-ninth person in the world to achieve the Grand Slam.

It took me two tries to bag a Rocky Mountain bighorn. It was during my first attempt that the unspeakable happened. My guide and I were literally camped in a cave close to six thousand feet up in the Canadian Rockies, just north of the Montana border, when two hijacked commercial jetliners slammed into the twin towers of the World Trade Center in New York. A third crashed into the Pentagon and a fourth in a Pennsylvania field. News of the epic tragedy reached us in drips. I had no idea of the scale of the disaster and the psychological damage it caused until we returned. Had I been home, I would have been glued to the TV and my cell phone, trying to fathom what had happened and to make certain friends or business associates traveling that day were unharmed. One guy I had known for years was a senior executive with a global investment firm headquartered in the Twin Towers. He and his wife lived in Manhattan and he walked to work most days. On the morning of September 11, he was delayed at home. When the news broke, the executive, who had been a Navy admiral, was on his way to work and knew immediately that the country was under attack by al-Qaeda. Most of the people in his firm died that day.

My guys at Armada Hoffler were also scrambling. Suddenly, providing security in our various high-rises and office buildings would mean more than posting security guards at entrances. I returned from the Rocky Mountains' sky tops to a different world.

CHAPTER XIV
Another Corner

"Life moves in phases. We don't necessarily want the same things in our forties and fifties that we did in our twenties and thirties."

Getting through the airports and home following the terrorist attacks was arduous but welcomed. Waiting for me was the new love in my life, my wife of nine months. I had met Valerie Adkins at the suggestion of some mutual friends. I didn't know much about her except that her dad, Howard, owned a chain of furniture stores and her mom, Maxine, owned a woman's dress boutique in a swanky section of Virginia Beach.

At age thirty-three, Valerie was quite a bit younger than me. It turns out we were born in the same hospital and delivered by the same doctor, but eighteen years apart. I saw the age difference as a plus. But she was, at least initially, cool to the idea of dating a twice-divorced older guy who by all accounts was an unabashed ladies' man.

Valerie had been dating and in and out of a couple of serious relationships. She was tired of "Peter Pans," boys who never wanted to grow up. I was looking for someone who was smart, independent, with a big heart and who could hold her own with governors, famous entertainers and rich CEOs, as well as regular folks. Valerie was poised beyond her years and elegant to boot.

Valerie initially rebuffed a friend's invitation to meet with me. After a second nudge several months later she relented, as long as it was a group date. There were five of us at dinner that August night in 1999, and Valerie and I didn't get to say much to each other. Every time I tried to speak to her, the other three at the table went silent. I knew Valerie was a clothes and fashion connoisseur, so I wore a gold Brioni suit. She looked stunning—a classic Northern European beauty with intelligent green eyes and a great smile. She was well-spoken, quick to laugh and seemed anything but intimidated. More than once she caught me staring at her feet, grinning only slightly to avoid embarrassing me or her. She would soon learn that I have a thing for pretty feet.

I really wanted to spend more time getting to know Valerie, and in a hurry, because I was about to leave the country for a month-long hunting expedition. So I called her the next day and asked if she would like to spend the afternoon at Point Farm and then, perhaps, join me for dinner. We hit it off right away, walking, talking and even buzzing around on a jet ski. We had a fun day and learned much more about each other over dinner.

She had attended a fashion and design college in Texas and returned to Virginia Beach to run a clothing boutique with her mom. Her father had done well selling furniture and built the business into eleven stores located in three states, providing

Valerie and her sisters a very comfortable life. Their world, however, would be shattered by a seemingly random tragedy. Valerie's oldest sister, Gwen, was a high school senior working at her father's Portsmouth furniture store. Typically, there were at least two people working at any time, but on this Tuesday night, Valerie's sister was alone. Valerie, who at the time was just six, went to the Portsmouth store with her mother and other sister, Jackie, to check in on Gwen. They found her on the floor behind the counter. The innocent high school girl had been shot and murdered during a robbery.

Valerie has an uncanny ability to remember dates and can recite the birthdays or anniversaries of scores of friends and family. The day she found her sister was seared into her memory. That profound loss would seed Valerie's appreciation for family and life. Valerie is elegant and proper, but she also has a great sense of humor and zest for having fun.

Valerie's mom, Maxine, remained protective of her little girl, and Valerie knew she would not approve of her dating a guy with four kids and an eye for women. Valerie kept mum about our day together at Point Farm and the following day, when she accompanied me to Richmond where I was catching a flight. As I entered the terminal, I tossed Valerie the keys to my Mercedes and asked her to drive it home for me.

I remained abroad for a month, but I called Valerie every day—literally every day. Valerie jokes that she knows what it is liked to be hunted by Dan Hoffler. We would talk for forty-five minutes to an hour. It was like an old-style courtship, where you get to know someone well before the relationship heats up. When I returned, I asked Valerie to join me at the Helmsley in New York for a show and dinner. I thought I would really impress her with two prime seats for "The Phantom of the Opera" on Broadway. She did a great job that night of hiding the fact that she had already seen the show twice before with two other boyfriends. I knew after that weekend in New York that our relationship was, as I told her, "a done deal." We were engaged in January 2000.

The best men in our wedding were my dad and my long-time friend and political ally Mark Warner, who was in hot pursuit of becoming Virginia's next governor. I had a close network of friends, a wonderful new bride and our construction and development business again was roaring. Life was good. What made it even better was that my kids took to Valerie, or as they call her, "VeeVee." She became a second mother to my boys and a friend and confidant to my daughters. She is also a phenomenal hostess and has a knack for assembling eclectic groups of people who all seem to click. And no one plans a party like Valerie or enjoys one more. She is nothing if not organized, a consummate list keeper. She slipped into my world as gracefully and effortlessly as silk on skin.

Ever since buying Point Farm I had considered building a new home at the far end of the property we call "the point," where Cherrystone flows join the Chesapeake Bay. There was a spot in the middle of pasture that yielded magnificent views of the creek to the south and the Bay to the north. The air moves more at that end of the farm, where breezes flow in off the Bay, keeping temperatures cooler in the summer. I put the word out to local fish houses, aqua farmers and contractors that I would take any crushed shells or fill dirt they needed to get rid of. Truckload by truckload came over several years until I had piles tall enough to start spreading. Once the material was packed and settled, it would make a great bed on which to build a house. I love Jefferson's Monticello and eighteenth-century Georgian architecture, so I commissioned an architect to design me a house replete with marble porch columns, a grand foyer, a hipped roof covered in slate, wrapped with lots of windows and porches to capture the views.

Valerie had been a good sport and moved in to the older house on the property after we were married. But we knew there were, as she puts it, "a lot of ghosts in that house." I had shown her the blueprint designs for the house of my dreams. Without her knowing it, I had the designs for the footprint of the house stretched from thirteen thousand square feet to twenty-five thousand. When I showed them to her, she was stunned. "Is this really an option?" she said.

It would take a year to get the structure designed and another two and a half years to build it. My friends jokingly referred to the house as "Valerie's starter home." It would become the largest home on the Shore, a fortress of marble, onyx, granite and slate with seven bedroom suites, ten bathrooms and two full kitchens. The exterior was a mass of brick and concrete sealed with windows that could repel even the most brutal hurricane. We designed an elevator and even a lookout station above the third floor. The two-story porch columns were made from marble dust and shipped by train from Chicago. Valerie and I traveled a lot when we were first together and in one year alone made nine trips abroad. We furnished the house from shops all over Europe along the way, which included a grand dining room table that seats sixteen. It was a shopping spree like no other, a monumental splurge that would require me to keep my day job for a while. We christened the house with a big celebration. The Farm was booked that evening with friends staying overnight and scores of others who came to see our new digs. Our voices grew sore giving "the tour." Valerie's starter home became a base camp for entertaining esteemed friends, such as the best man at our wedding.

CHAPTER XV
A Good Cause

"When you have a received a lot in life, it's important
to give something back. This was an opportunity for
me to get involved in a cause I believed in."

Mark Warner rolled into the governor's mansion by
breaking a sweat. He was an exhaustive campaigner who raised
lots of cash and kicked in a chunk of his own to finance his
run. Mark and his opponent, another fellow named Mark, the
state's attorney general, kept the fight clean. There was no name
calling or bullying, no spies secretly taping meetings or rallies,
and no demonizing the opposition. By all accounts, the other
Mark was a nice guy and a deeply devout Christian. However,
Mark was the kind of politician Virginian's liked—a fiscally
moderate businessman who was comfortable with gun owners
and the law and order crowd, but who didn't use the podium as
a pulpit. Mark believed, and still does, that government should
stay out of people's personal lives. He also felt that a state, like

a business, needed to spend wisely and keep its books balanced.

Mark was like several of the people I had connected with and grown close to. He was a self-made guy who came from a modest background. He was the first in his family to graduate college and had the same level of can-do determination and energy I had seen in Doug Wilder. Mark was Doug's campaign manager and Mark and I had worked hand in hand to get him elected governor.

Mark had made a fortune as a young guy investing in the then fledgling cell phone business. And his success was no accident or streak of luck. This was one smart guy and a real competitor.

Mark was one of those annoying types who didn't need to study much to make A's. He breezed through his Connecticut high school and did the same at George Washington University, where he finished first in his class with a perfect grade point average. Mark loved politics and while in school worked on political campaigns, often missing classes. He apologized to his professors for being absent, did the reading on his own and then aced the exams. He whizzed through Harvard Law School with much the same ease, and he didn't even want to be a lawyer.

Mark returned to Washington to join the staff of a U.S. senator. While doing committee work, Mark saw the potential in a new telephone technology. Using towers, like radio stations, people would no longer have to be tethered to a phone line to make a call. The federal government could sell licenses for mobile phone franchises and companies with deep pockets could build cell phone networks.

Mark got in on the ground floor and with some investors bought a bunch of the licenses and then brokered them. He was also an early investor in Nextel, which was based in the Washington suburb of Reston, Virginia. Nextel would eventually merge with Sprint.

Mark was a cool guy with tons of energy and a deep streak of civility instilled in him by his parents, who had grown up in the Midwest. He was decent, honest and liked to win, rarely giving up a chance to play a pickup game of basketball or debate policy. He was a wonk and a jock who could be deadpan serious one moment and share a joke the next.

Mark was an early financial supporter of Doug and had been tapped to coordinate his gubernatorial campaign in northern Virginia. Those first months of Doug's bid were bumpy, and Doug was not happy with how his schedule was being handled. The final straw was added to his frustration at an event in Virginia Beach. Doug attended what he thought was supposed to be a debate with his opponent. Instead, the venue turned into a mauling by a member of the press asking questions. Doug was furious. After the event, Mark and Doug joined me at my beach house. It was clear to Doug and I that we needed to make some changes, so with some very mild arm twisting, we asked Mark to take over as Doug's campaign manager.

The newly elected governor appointed Mark and I to the Commonwealth Transportation Board. It wasn't the most exciting work, but Mark and I took it seriously and attended the board's many meetings. We started hanging out together, getting a couple of drinks or dinner after the board sessions ended.

Mark and I evolved from allies into friends. We were both nouveau riche trying to find our place. "Neither of us knew if the establishment would accept us," Mark says. "We were kindred spirits in that way." We were also friendly competitors who liked to tease each other and share a laugh. I taunted Mark about his frumpy Brooks Brothers look. He was lanky and thin and his clothes seemed to hang on him like a bedsheet on a clothesline.

He fired back by calling me a peacock with my tailored Italian suits.

We started hanging out together and even did a couple of business deals. Our most public partnership was in 1997 when we chipped in to help actors Tim and Daphne Maxwell Reid start New Millennium Studios. Tim and Daphne had starred in several successful TV sitcoms, and wanted to bring a touch of Hollywood to Virginia. The New Millennium campus provided a boom for Petersburg, which had been a somewhat depressed small city just south of the state capital of Richmond. At the time, the moviemakers were looking for cheaper venues to make films, and we figured our little studio could be part of that, especially for historical documentaries set in Virginia. It was a fun but expensive investment that neither of us profited from. To this day, Mark says getting into the deal was my idea, but I like blaming him. Either way, I enjoyed the glitz and learned a few things about moviemaking.

Mark was a natural politician with broad appeal. He was a hugely successful businessman, which gave him credibility with the pro-business crowd, and a policy wonk who had the brains and interest to dissect the most complex issues. He helped make history getting Doug Wilder elected and decided to jump into the fray as a frontman. Mark did a warm-up run for a U.S. Senate seat against Virginia's invincible Republican incumbent, John Warner. The two Warners were not related but treated each other as though they were kin. Both men had kind things to say about each other and both were very much moderates, so there wasn't much room for criticism.

Mark did well enough to become his party's choice for governor, and I was proud to be a big supporter of my friend. I stood near the podium with him when he took the oath of office and spent many nights as his overnight guest in the Executive Mansion. Knowing of my interest in conservation and hunting,

Mark appointed me to the board of the state Department of Game and Inland Fisheries, known as DGIF. I had served on several state boards, but the July 2002 appointment to the game department truly excited me. Like on most state boards, those appointed serve for free. And serving on the board certainly wasn't going to enhance my development or construction business. None of that mattered. I truly felt that working with the agency was a way to serve the state in an area that I cared about deeply. It was a good cause.

I had come to know a fair amount about the agency through my friend Mike Caison, the Eastern Shore game warden, and about game laws and animal populations. The agency had, in my view, been significantly underfunded for years, was overworked and battled with low morale. The Game Department was operating on forty-five million a year with no money coming from the state's general fund. The agency lived off of hunting and fishing licensing fees and taxes collected from outdoor equipment sales. The expansive Eastern Shore at times had just a couple of men trying to police and monitor its thousands of acres of shoreline, forests and fields. A stunning lack of manpower was true elsewhere in the state. It also seemed wrong that game wardens were not considered law enforcement officers, at least not when it came to pay. Many wardens with a decade of experience were making salaries in the low thirty thousands, which was a third less than state police officers. Some warden's salaries were so low that they met federal and state definitions of poverty. Yet a lot of their duties and skills and the risks they took were similar to local and state police. In the course of a day, a game warden might chase down illegal hunters in remote areas, or participate in nighttime sting operations to bust poachers illegally setting traps or bait, or find a missing hunter wandering around lost in a swamp. Their work rarely makes the big headlines of urban or suburban crime, but it can be just as risky of a business, often without much reward.

Turnover was high in Virginia's DGIF and accelerated after the terrorist attacks in 2001 as game wardens left the agency for better paying work in the exploding law enforcement field. There were only about one hundred and sixty or so wardens in the field spread over the entire state to begin with. They were spread even thinner even as farms turned into huge subdivisions overrun with deer and other critters now out of a home.

One of my goals going into the job was to help infuse some pride into the ranks by getting the agency reclassified from a Level III agency to Level I, the same as state police. After months of intense lobbying and support from the governor, Virginia's House of Delegates and the Senate voted overwhelmingly to upgrade DGIF's classification. Mike Caison had been named legislative liaison by his bosses and was the agency's point man on that effort, holding countless meetings with lawmakers to press the case.

As part of our agenda, I also wanted to help modernize the agency with new equipment and innovative enforcement techniques. Law breakers, such as poachers, were getting harder to catch and there were more of them. There was a lucrative market for rare animals or animal parts and, like drug runners, poachers were using increasingly sophisticated methods to ply their trade. Asian medicine makers were paying four thousand dollars or more for the thumb-sized gall bladder cut out of Virginia black bears or for bear paws. Fish poachers were also taking prized catches to sell on the black market. The agency just couldn't keep up.

The connection between "conservation" and "hunting" had become abundantly clear to me. You can't have one without the other. Anti-hunting groups don't seem to understand—or simply will not accept—that animal populations must be managed and protected, to survive. We no longer live in the wide-open prairies and forests. The amount of living space for animals has decreased as the number of people has exploded. It's true that sport hunters kill animals that might otherwise live. But it's also true that loss of habitat, commercial hunting and poaching take a far greater toll. That's a fact in this country and just about everywhere else in the world.

Game laws are intended to protect and manage species. Ironically, fees for hunting licenses and permits to cull them pay a big chunk of the freight. Without fees paid by hunters, fishermen and trappers, there wouldn't be much money for wildlife protection. Hunters, at least those I have been around, understand the connection. Those with money also make big contributions to land conservation groups and those with land, like farmers, plant crops and rows of dense vegetation to feed and hide otherwise vulnerable critters.

Anti-hunting groups tend to focus on the "rights" of an individual animal. True conservationists focus on sustaining the whole. Animal populations are closely monitored by men and women with advanced degrees in science. They carefully calculate the size of a herd or flock and balance that with the food and living resources available. Hunting quotas are then set, based on the science. The balance can be thrown off-kilter when politics trumps science.

There are plenty of examples where prohibiting hunting has backfired, as there are plenty of instances of allowing too many of a species to be harvested. Unrestricted commercial fishing has decimated some fish populations. Cutting it back, especially in places like the Chesapeake Bay, has helped striped bass and blue crab populations rebound.

I remember when there was a multi-year ban on hunting snow geese. Their numbers had crashed following a few years of drought on the tundra, which is where they return to breed every year. The population recovered as breeding conditions improved, leading to a population explosion. As a result, swarms of the hungry geese devoured wetlands and vegetation needed for food and protection by other birds, causing those populations to crash. If you study conservation, you quickly learn that too many of a species can be as bad as too few. Too many foxes can wipe out rabbits or quail. Too many nutria destroy wetlands, and so on.

After a year, I was appointed chairman of the DGIF board. By then, I had spent a lot of time in the field with the director, top officers and wardens and felt I had a pretty strong handle on the politics of the agency. I wanted to be more than a talking head in a suit, so I started attending seminars and witnessing field operations. In the past, DGIF board members took more passive roles. It was a quiet agency that rarely received much attention.

As chairman, I was much more hands-on than some in the agency were used to. I had learned a lot about managing and protecting large animals on my various hunting trips to Africa, where the battle with poachers can be lethal and the tactics on both sides of the war are very sophisticated. I also did what I could financially to help the agency as well. I bought it some very expensive equipment, including a remote-controlled decoy deer used to trap poachers. I paid some travel expenses for officials to attend workshops. I bought the agency ATVs, helped with the expenses of boats and loaned one of my docks at Point Farm to game officials so they would have a place to tie up patrol boats. I also introduced the agency director and his assistants to some of the most influential lawmakers and business people and raised the agency's profile in the governor's office, which helped us to get the agency reclassified. More than once, top DGIF officials attended an annual dove shoot I hosted, mostly to mingle with others and represent the agency. I had no idea then how badly good intentions can backfire.

CHAPTER XVI
Standing Firm

"A lot of people who think they know about conservation really don't understand it."

As with just about everything in my life, one challenge entices me to attempt an even bigger one. My trips hunting mountain sheep to achieve the North American "Grand Slam" stoked my burn to achieve the African "Big Five." Not many people in the world can go on safari because not many can afford it. The nations of Africa have become extremely restrictive, especially when it comes to trophy hunting, and they closely regulate how many animals can be culled a year and where.

The same forces that drive animal populations and threaten them in the United States are at play in Africa, except it is more deadly. Poaching and land development have crashed the numbers of the most coveted five African game species: lions, rhinoceroses, elephants, Cape buffaloes and leopards. Poachers are much more aggressive and will kill people who interfere. They're basically order fillers profiting from a black market for rare animal skins, horns or body parts. Like Mexican drug dealers, poachers are often well-financed and use helicopters, ATVs and communication satellites. They pay off law enforcers and others and even use villagers as spies and agents.

I got a crash course on big game economics while in South Africa. Basically, the country has been able to thwart poaching and stabilize animal populations with a free market approach. They license private and public lands to companies that manage them and make money at it by charging people like me a lot to hunt. The income enables these preserve managers to hire security and buy equipment needed to battle poachers. They also employ biologists who carefully monitor populations and survival conditions.

The biggest conservation success story in South Africa is the Pongola Game Reserve. Back in the 1980s, poachers and farmers nearly wiped out dozens of big game species. Swaths of savannah were fenced off for cattle, limiting food and water for roaming wild animals. It finally clicked that there was potentially more wealth in hosting travelers than in selling steers, so land owners and farmers tore down fences and partnered with the government to restore the great predators and grazers that had become synonymous with Africa.

By the early 2000s, when I traveled to Pongola, the region had restored nearly all of the indigenous animal populations. Wildlife biologists systematically maximized their reproduction and survival. As part of that system, a few—very few—of the rarest big game animals could be culled each year. In most cases, it was mature males well beyond their peak years as breeders. Some rhinos have lived five decades and even though they're no longer potent breeders, they'll scare off younger, more viral males.

Keeping the bloodline fresh has helped restore Africa's white rhinos and its rarer black cousins. Both are really gray, but

Rhino taken during one of my African safari hunts. This animal charged me and
dropped just yards away on my second shot.

The Shaw Group CEO Jim Bernhard
and I in Spain

One of the four bighorn sheep I took to
achieve the coveted Grand Slam

This leopard, taken during an African safari, was poised to attack and just a few yards away.

My sons, Hunter and Daniel, with me after a swan hunt in North Carolina.

My sons, Hunter and Daniel, with me after a turkey hunt on Virginia's Eastern Shore.

have different shaped lips. White rhinos are the larger and more numerous of the two. They can stand six feet at the shoulders, be twelve feet long and weigh two-to-three tons. Their horns are rings of hardened hair that grow solid like tree trunks. The lower of the two horns, the thing that tempts poachers, can grow to five feet. Asian and Arab cultures pay tens of thousands for the horns, which they grind up and sell as a mystical form of Viagra to men. Arab carvers make ornaments with them. Poaching remains the biggest threat to these beasts.

Pongola allowed only two white rhinos to be taken in 2004. The privilege of taking one of them cost me seventy-five thousand dollars. Few people in the world have achieved the Big Five of game hunting, and price is a main reason why. Nothing is free on these trips. There are fees for every animal taken, depending on their rarity. It sounds crass to sell animals by make and model, the way dealerships sell cars, but this free market system provides Pongola and places like it with income to pay the legions of biologists, veterinarians and game wardens that manage and care for these herds. Sightseers and hunters fill lodges and restaurants and hire guides too.

The Pongola reserve feels like Jurassic Park. The size and number of free-roaming animals is exhilarating. There are more than three hundred species that graze in the grasslands, hide in the cliffs and forests, and congregate at the watering holes and along riverbeds. The animals are closely observed, so the guides are pretty certain where they will be most days and the best times to get close. They also know which specific animals to take. You only shoot when they tell you.

Finding a white rhino on the preserve is one thing. Getting within range of a large male takes some nerve and luck. Rhinos are deceptively keen, swift and dangerous. Their vision is poor, but they more than compensate with hearing and smell. You have to stay downwind to get near one. If they get to you first, their horns and thick skull can flatten or gore you like a knife into a watermelon. They've been known to punch holes in cars.

The ammunition of choice for a rhino is a .470 Nitro Express. Firing one of these is like shooting a small missile. The bullet is four inches long, almost the size of a fountain pen. Recoil can break a shoulder and the bullet can split a tree. Most guns that fire this caliber are bolt action with one heavy, thick barrel. I decided on a two-shot Purdey double rifle, a thirteen-pound lethal monster. I had practiced firing it, literally bracing my body and shoulder so the recoil wouldn't knock me on my butt. You definitely think about the kick before pulling the trigger. It'll rattle your brain.

It was a May afternoon, around dusk. There were several people in the hunting party, including a guide and videographer. An old bull had been spotted and we were stalking quietly through some scrubby brush and trees. Sure enough, a large male came ambling through, less than thirty yards away, slowly walking and munching. He was easily over two tons and his long horn appeared at least two feet. The guide signaled me to take the shot. The best way to take down a rhino is to shoot him behind the shoulder so that the bullet reaches his heart or lungs. Their skulls are so thick that bullets can bounce off, so head shots can be useless unless you're just a few feet away, which isn't recommended.

My first shot grazed a branch and ripped into the rhino's chest. Instead of dropping, he turned menacingly and charged. The videographer shouted and ran, and the guide scaled a tree, tearing skin off of his arm and legs. I heard the scurrying and yelling but kept my eyes fixed on the rhino barreling toward me. I told myself to stay calm and to focus, picking out a spot on the part of the beast in clearest view—his massive skull. The bullet did its job, collapsing the animal fifteen feet in front of me. I didn't feel my heart pounding or legs quivering until after the bull hit the ground.

CHAPTER XVII
Good Intentions Gone Bad

"I made a mistake. I should never have put myself or
those guys in the line of fire."

The trip to Pongola in the spring of 2004 had been so
invigorating that I planned on returning to neighboring
Zimbabwe in the fall. I thought it would be educational and fun
for my friend Mike and his bosses, DGIF Director Bill Woodfin
and his chief of law enforcement, Terry Bradbery, to join me.
Mike, who had been promoted to assistant law enforcement
chief by then, and others in the agency had ratcheted up the
number of undercover operations to nab poachers, so I figured
they could learn a few tricks from the professionals in Africa.
They also had some population management scientists that I
thought we could learn from.

Virginia law requires cabinet level approval anytime state
officials travel abroad for business, so I asked the Secretary of
Natural Resources, who oversees DGIF, for permission, which

his office granted. With that, I booked the trip, paying all of my own expenses, plus travel and lodging costs for Bill, Mike and Terry. They would only need some time away from the office and appropriate apparel.

Word about the safari trickled out after Bill, Mike and Terry bought some boots, walking sticks, khakis and electronic equipment with state credit cards. It was routine for agency officials to use the credit cards to buy materials or gear they needed for work, including uniforms, and anything they purchased remained the property of the state. That was SOP for the agency. In all, the three men spent about eleven thousand, five hundred dollars, which included a satellite phone the director could use when in remote areas and away from the office. The other gear would also be worn or used on official business when the men were in the field back in Virginia.

With less than two weeks before the Zimbabwe trip, word came down that the office of the Secretary of Natural Resources had reversed its decision. It would not sanction the safari as official Virginia business. At that point, everything was paid for, and, honestly, I was upset. It seemed wrong to sabotage the trip with such short notice, especially after we had already been given permission. So we decided to make the trip unofficial. The three DGIF leaders would use vacation time. In hindsight, that was a bad decision. Bill Woodfin and I should have anticipated the backlash from basically thumbing our noses at the higher-ups. I should never have put myself or those guys in the line of fire.

The trip proved eye-opening for the guys. Mike went out on patrol with game wardens who caught poachers in the act. The African wardens weren't messing around and were ready to shoot the intruders. One warden told Mike to shoot, who of course, refused.

Not long after we returned, the trip turned into a political hailstorm. Some disgruntled wardens in the department had been stewing since earlier in the year when four DGIF employees were disciplined after an all-terrain vehicle accident left one warden severely injured. Terry had disciplined them for not wearing safety helmets. Others within the agency were, in my view, jealous that Mike and possibly others were removed from the field and placed in administrative roles. Some suggested I was benefiting somehow by allowing game wardens to moor patrol boats and store some equipment at my farm. And others complained about game wardens attending my dove shoots on the Shore. I thought I was doing the agency a favor, saving it some money and raising its profile, but I can now see how cynics can spin good intentions into something bad. The Zimbabwe mistake erupted into a brutal lesson in how appearances can trump reality.

A pair of disgruntled private citizens unwittingly lit the fuse that led to all the grief. A husband and wife from the western end of the state were upset that the agency had closed a fish hatchery to visitors for financial reasons. The couple, using public document laws, wanted to challenge the decision by proving that the agency was wasting money elsewhere. The safari would be their smoking gun.

The couple got the documents and provided them to the Richmond, Virginia, newspaper, which published a long and accusatory story. That, in turn, provoked state auditors to investigate. I never saw this coming, and to this day I contend that there was nothing unethical—and certainly not illegal—about the Africa trip or the tens of thousands of dollars' worth of equipment I had gifted to the agency. I certainly did not benefit—not one cent—from serving on the board.

When the news hit, I immediately moved to reimburse the state for any charges on state credit cards that were even remotely connected to the seventeen-day Zimbabwe trip. The state would not be out a penny. The state auditor's report painted a damning and highly exaggerated picture of cronyism, waste and discontent within the department. The auditor never once attempted to interview me, Mike, Bill or Terry. It was, in my view, an overt political attack based on perceptions and innuendo, not facts or motivation.

Anybody who thinks being connected to people in high places insulates you from scrutiny probably watches too much TV. My connection to the governor and to the attorney general stoked what would quickly turn into a three-year witch hunt. Mark Warner did not intervene in any manner and, in fact, distanced himself from the scandal. The state attorney general did the same. It would have been inappropriate for either man to do otherwise, and I would never ask them to compromise themselves.

I had contributed a lot of money to Virginia Attorney General Bob McDonnell, a Republican. The auditor's report had stirred up the press, which was clamoring for blood. Detractors and newspaper opinion writers accused McDonnell of stonewalling. The innuendo was that campaign contributions bought political favor, or at least it looked that way. Bob ultimately recused himself and handed the decision to prosecute off to an assistant. Bob did what he had to do, and I respect that.

However, I believe to this day that the DGIF witch hunt was politically motivated. It was, in my view, an attempt to hurt Mark Warner by discrediting me. I can't prove it, but that is what I was told by credible people, both Republicans and Democrats. They thought I had been wrongfully tarnished and that spending three years prosecuting Mike, Bill and Terry was a travesty. When you look at the facts and weigh them against the zeal of state prosecutors, it's hard to think otherwise. Mark's tenure as governor had gone very well. Virginia had been stressed financially from the recession and a series of tax cuts that depleted revenues. Mark got the state back on track fiscally and preserved Virginia's AAA municipal bond rating, which is the gold standard of credit worthiness. He was increasingly being discussed as presidential timber, a moderate who would appeal to both parties. At the very least, he was viewed as an almost unbeatable candidate for the U.S. Senate. Bringing me down would have been a stain on Mark's administration and his reputation.

After several failed attempts, prosecutors finally persuaded a grand jury to do its bidding. Mike Caison and Bill Woodfin were indicted on two counts each for misusing state money and Terry Bradbery on one charge. The men each faced ten years in jail for each count and huge fines. I was not indicted because I did not have a state credit card, spent no state money and never asked to be reimbursed. Fact is, I had spent more than one hundred thousand dollars of personal funds to help DGIF and I had paid out of my own pocket for all travel, lodging, gratuities and meals for the Zimbabwe trip.

Even before a single allegation was proven, Bill, Terry and Mike's careers were ruined. Bill resigned his post within weeks of the auditor's report and Mike and Terry were on leave and would eventually decide to retire. All three men had dedicated their lives to protecting wildlife. It was sickening and sad to see how perceptions and innuendo ruined them. Mike had been hunting with his brother out West when he received a phone call advising him that he needed to report to Virginia state police to be fingerprinted and booked. Mike arrived home within a couple days and surrendered himself. The state police officers were apologetic as they booked him and placed him in a holding cell.

I had resigned as chairman, primarily because the criticisms of me would hurt the agency and remain a distraction. I didn't have to resign and Mark did not ask me to do so. Even so, pundits and opinion writers speculated that I had been spared prosecution because of political connections, which turned out to be the irony of all ironies. It was the most hurtful and infuriating time of my life. My integrity and honesty had been skewed; my reputation was being trampled; these men I had tried to help were called criminals.

Lawyers and others with an informed view of the charges and legal proceedings assured me that the indictments were based on a case so thin, so presumptuous and petty, that it should never have gone to court. Any thoughtful judge would toss the case, I was told. True as that might be, the men charged still had to defend themselves.

The case lingered for nearly three excruciating years. The state attorney general's office spent tens of thousands of dollars and ultimately wound up embarrassing itself. The office insisted on trying each of the men separately, which meant three trials. Defense lawyers wanted to expedite the matter in one case to spare the men the expense and agony of protracted litigation.

First up was Mike. Midway through the case, the presiding Richmond Circuit Court judge stopped the trial and threw out the two embezzlement charges. The judge ruled that the state did not prove that Mike had committed a crime. Mike's lawyers never even had to put on a defense. A month later, the state dropped the charge against Terry, because the evidence against him was even shabbier. Finally, another circuit judge hearing the case against Bill threw out the charges two hours before the trial was to begin. The judge ruled that the state had no facts to prove that the former DGIF director knowingly broke the law. Moments after the case was tossed out, Bill's attorney, Joseph Owen III, told the media what I had been feeling all along. The entire episode had been a travesty.

"From the first time I looked at this I could not figure out why anyone would view this as a criminal action," Owen said. "Mr. Woodfin dedicated thirty years of his life to public service, and he was paid back with indictments.... He has been acquitted, but at the very least has had two or three years of his life taken from him worrying about this crap."

Nothing ever happened to the overzealous prosecutors or their supervisors who pressed the case. There was never an apology issued by the attorney general's office or media pundits. In fact, the office remained arrogant and stalwart even with its embarrassing defeats, defending its decision to prosecute as "crucial to the public trust in government." In my view, witch hunts driven by political motivation erode the public's trust in government.

CHAPTER XVIII
Nanuq

"These animals are not going to run.
You're their food."

I refused to allow the DGIF episode zap my enthusiasm
for hunting and conservation. As I have learned over and over
again, the best way to deal with setbacks is to get them behind
you and move on. There was yet another hunting challenge I
wanted to conquer, the most arduous of all.

Nanuq, the Inuit word for polar bear, is the animal at the
very top of the food chain and the earth. It had taken more than a
year to arrange the trip and a week just to reach the Inuit village
of Cambridge. Our first plane stop was in Edmonton, Alberta.
Next stop, Yellowknife, a town of about twenty thousand and
the capital and largest city of the Northwest Territories. Just two
hundred and fifty miles south of the Arctic Circle, Yellowknife
has a front seat to the Northern Lights and hails itself as the

diamond capital of the world.

The weather that far north in April can be bitter and dangerous, even though it's technically spring. Sub-zero temperatures and cyclones can kill you in seconds and bring down planes. When the weather finally cooperated, we continued north into Cambridge, part of an archipelago entombed in ice most of the year.

To find Cambridge on a map, draw a straight line north from North Dakota until you reach Nunavut, which lies within the Arctic Circle above the sixtieth parallel. Nunavut used to be part of the Northwest Territories and was carved off and deeded to the Inuit as part of reparations made by the Canadian government to native people. It's hard to understand the desolation of this region. Its land mass is as large as Greenland and is bigger than Texas, California, Montana and New Mexico combined. Only thirty-two thousand people are spread over more than seven hundred thousand acres. Cambridge, the last sizeable outpost, has only about a thousand residents. Most are Inuit who hunt and fish for food and live in what most Americans would consider shacks. Diesel generators provide all of their power and animal skins keep them warm.

There is no economy to speak of. Most of the people live off the land. There are some mining jobs, but digging for gold, nickel, copper or diamonds isn't steady work because the ground stays frozen most of the time. One thing that has given the villagers a boost is sport hunting. Rich guys like me pay big bucks to hunt polar bears. The bears are protected and their populations closely monitored. Canada issues a limited number of polar bear hunting permits each year to its indigenous people. To bring in much needed income, some of the villages, like Cambridge, sell two-to-three permits a year to trophy hunters, who are escorted by Inuit guides on expeditions. I paid fifty thousand dollars for a permit and about another twenty grand on transportation and the hunt itself. I had spent thousands on the most sophisticated hunting clothing made from the most scientific fabrics and materials too. I quickly discovered that the high-tech stuff doesn't keep you warm in temperatures that routinely drop to thirty below zero. The best way to keep from freezing is to wrap up in caribou skins and wear them on your hands and head, just like the Inuit.

There's basically two ways to get around in this part of the world, by dogsleds or less-reliable snowmobiles. We had both. I rode on the bed of a dogsled stuffed inside a coffin-like box with only my head sticking out. My guide, Willie, was the musher and stood behind me steering the dogs and scanning the blinding white horizon. Sunlight reflecting on the ice often threw off prisms of blues, yellows, reds and greens. I may have well as been on another planet.

We had set up a base camp of tents and supplies, where, with any luck, we would return each day after sledding and stalking for up to fourteen hours. It was light most of the day, and even though I sat tucked in a box, the extreme weather and long hours left me exhausted and nearly delirious each night.

I was warned about the "whiteouts" but really had no idea of their ferocity until I had to urinate in the middle of the night. The wind howled so loud I could not hear what my tent mate, just a few feet away, was saying. People, even seasoned natives, have died in whiteouts just a few yards from their homes. There's no distinction between the sky and ground. Everything is exactly the same, like being in complete darkness. There are no visual markers to guide you in any direction and no sound other than screaming winds. I had become disoriented after taking just a couple of steps out of the tent. Fortunately, I felt my way back inside, but I never ventured into a storm again without tethering myself with a rope line to the tent. Even when the winds aren't blasting, it's so cold your pee freezes instantly.

The Inuit speak about the power of dreams. They say dying on the ice is a peaceful and dignified way to leave the world. You simply slip into a dreamlike state without pain or anguish. Scientists put a different spin on it. Hypothermia can induce vivid dreams because of the way a cold brain and body distribute blood flow. Whatever the explanation, I had the most vivid and peaceful sleeping experience of my life one night when the temperatures plunged.

I slept in a sleeping bag laid over caribou skins, fully clothed and with a Russian-style fur hat with ear covers. The hat had fallen off while I slept. It was Christmas day and I was a young boy sitting by the tree opening presents with my sister, Sharon. She looked pretty and young as did Mother and Father. We were laughing and joking and joyous. The bulbs on the Christmas tree were sparkling with different colors. The presents were wrapped in bright paper with bows. I felt peaceful and basked in the happiness of being a kid again. I don't know how long the dream lasted or what it meant in any metaphysical sense. But I know it felt real and that it was like I had lived it. I have never had a dream so vivid since.

There was no shortage of bears in the area. Willie had spotted several, but they were mostly small males, sows or cubs. Despite having free rein, the Inuit are careful to cull just mature males. They, in my view, understand bear behaviors and populations better than scientists because Inuit live among the animals. Inuit are not oblivious to warming weather patterns and shifts in ice floes. They study the movement of bears not out of academic curiosity, but because their livelihoods depend on it. Inuit also have a spiritual connection with the bears. The spirit of a cull "nanuq" taken honorably and without suffering will, essentially, spread the word among the living bears that the hunter is an honorable person worthy of surrendering their life too.

The polar bear I shot on my second trip to the Arctic

Willie and I had hunted for several days and finally came upon some bears that looked large enough to consider. The wind was howling and snow was blowing, somewhat obscuring our view. Willie instructed me to shoot what appeared to be a mid-sized male about eight feet tall. When we approached the downed animal, Willie immediately realized he had made a grave mistake. We had killed a sow, and not a very large one at that.

Willie was mortified. We broke camp that day, taking our half-ton mistake with us. When we returned to Cambridge, Willie was so ashamed that he disappeared for several days, soaking away his torment. The village leaders had the animal skinned and butchered for food because wasting it would be a far greater offense. But they did so with remorse. Disgraced and embarrassed, they invited me to return the next spring and would give me another permit. I took them up on their offer and replayed the journey the following April, once again with Willie as my guide.

An international debate had been brewing about the plight of the polar bear in the mid-to-late 2000s. By some scientific counts, there were fewer than 25,000 wild polar bears roaming the North. Many attributed the dwindling populations to global warming. Without thick ice to traverse, there was less range for the bears to hunt, and these animals require a lot of fish, seals and other meat to live. "Ice bear" can grow to more than a half ton and live two decades. One science group predicted two-thirds of the bears would be wiped out by global warming. The United States responded by declaring the polar bear a "threatened" species. As such, imports of polar bear skins and trophies would be banned starting May 2008. I would be one of the last Americans to hunt polar bears with the Inuit.

Starting each day from base camp in a similar location to that of the previous year, Willie and I set out on a dogsled once again. And, once again, we saw a lot of bears and endured bitter cold. We were about a week into the trip when Willie spotted a large male about thirty yards away. It was a frantic few moments. It was so cold, my hands were numb. I slid my rifle from inside the coffin-like box and took aim through a scope. I had no feeling in my trigger hand, which was like a hunk of ice on the end of my arm. While I shifted the gun into position, it fired. I had pulled the trigger without knowing it. The bullet hit the bear's leg, leaving a bloody trail as he hobbled off. The animal paused and thankfully I had a second chance. He was a monster, standing over ten feet, one of the largest Willie had seen. We celebrated that night, and Willie felt vindicated.

It took months, tons of phone calls and a mountain of paperwork to get my trophy home. As for Willie and the Inuit of Cambridge, their guide business quickly vanished. I spoke to Willie after the import ban was in place. "Protecting" polar bears from trophy hunters like me seemed to be having the opposite effect. Without the money from hunting permit sales, the people of Cambridge didn't have the income to buy supplies and import food, so they resorted to what they had done for generations—killing and eating polar bears. Instead of taking just a few bears a year, they were now killing more than twenty.

CHAPTER XIX
Town Center

"They said it was a pipe-dream."

For almost as long as Armada Hoffler had been in business, there was talk about the need for a real downtown in Virginia Beach. The state's most populated city had grown from the outside in. The Chesapeake Bay wraps the city to its north, the Atlantic Ocean to the east and North Carolina to the south. Like much of Hampton Roads, the Beach is rife with creeks and rivers that, on a map, look like an artery with veins. The affluent long ago claimed the best waterfront spots, and the Navy grabbed the rest. Its East Coast master jet base sits in the middle of the city, and the storied Navy Seals have a base on the Bay. Large swaths of ocean and Bay beach are fenced off and controlled by the service.

Virginia Beach is strewn with a scattered mix of shopping districts and malls, car dealerships, supermarkets, furniture stores and fast-food joints. In all, four hundred and fifty thousand people live here in everything from packed subdivisions of townhouses and apartments, to sprawling neighborhoods of brick ranch houses, to cliques of million dollar, waterfront homes tucked along shaded cul-de-sacs.

The hot spot at the Beach is its Oceanfront, lined with hotels, trinket shops, restaurants and bars. The "strip," as it is called, is packed during the summer with sailors and tourists cruising the Boardwalk and Atlantic and Pacific avenues. Tourism and the military fuel the Beach's economy. Compared to neighboring cities in Hampton Roads, and pretty much throughout Virginia, the Beach is pretty well-heeled. It has a low tax rate, low crime, great schools and a higher than average per capita income. Most of Hampton Roads is, at least statistically, a meat-and-potatoes market. Walmart, Kmart and other big-box discounters love the region. The Beach had been lumped into that category too, making it difficult, if not impossible, to attract high-end retailers.

For all of its people and wealth, the Beach lacked what most cities of distinction rely upon—a central downtown business district. Norfolk has one, replete with an upscale shopping mall. But the Beach's business base had been spread over its four hundred and ninety-seven square miles of suburbia, water and open space. Nearly all shopping and working in the Beach had been based on driving from one strip mall to the next.

A small group of Beach business people, led by local real estate property manager Gerald Divaris, bucked the stereotypes of the Beach back in the late 1980s by pushing for a pedestrian friendly downtown. The vision included tall office buildings, an upscale shopping center and a selection of great high-end restaurants and bars. Gerald saw the diamonds hidden beneath a pile of statistics about the region. The Beach was actually affluent by most standards. A chunk of the city's residents are retired military who finished their service after twenty years and then entered the civilian workforce, earning a salary as they also collect a military pension. The city's population also spends about twenty percent more on shopping than the national average. Gerald drilled into the numbers and discovered that the Beach's household income was actually about thirty percent higher than national figures suggested.

After years of fierce lobbying, city leaders got on board. They created a central business district in 1976 that would encompass fifteen hundred acres smack in the middle of the city. There were already a couple of office buildings there, an old mall and some fast-food places, but much of the space was woods, and better yet it was flanked by the city's main east-west artery and the Interstate. It was another Greenbrier waiting for a developer.

The city and Gerald tried repeatedly to launch the district. It seemed like every year or so there was yet another false start. A developer or investors would sniff around, or Gerald would think he had some fancy retailers lined up. But for various reasons the plans stalled or were abandoned. Newspaper opinion writers and naysayers seemed to revel in these false starts, constantly poking fun at Gerald's dream and admonishing the city to stop wasting its time. It was a pipe-dream, pie in the sky. It would never work. The area already had a downtown Norfolk, so why another one? Gerald shrugged off the unrelenting mocking and persisted.

We had been pretty happy in our six-floor Chesapeake office, and the city had been great to Armada Hoffler. But there had been a mood swing in Chesapeake as members of its council no longer seemed as encouraging to business growth. As a company, we were also getting restless. We had hit another boom cycle and were now doing massive high-profile projects in urban centers elsewhere in the new millennium. We had even, at one point, talked about setting up a headquarters outside the region, perhaps around Washington or Baltimore.

Lou had met Gerald Divaris on a couple of occasions. We had done plenty of business at the Beach and were familiar with the city's pro-business, smart-growth leadership. Lou met with Gerald and then approached Russ and I. "I think this can work. I think this can be a good thing for us," he said. The Beach's central business district was in a perfect location, eleven miles down a highway from Norfolk and eleven miles in the other direction to the Oceanfront.

Some of the previous proposals for a Beach downtown failed because they were too ambitious and expensive. They called for five hundred million dollars' worth of development in one gulp. In almost every case, they were developers from elsewhere not completely familiar with the region, which made the concept an even tougher sell. A skidding economy had also scuttled a couple of proposals, spooking lenders. High-end retailers were also skittish because the downtown envisioned was still nothing more than ideas on paper. They wanted to see some sidewalks, parking garages and office buildings before they would take a chance.

The problem, as we saw it, was the scale of the project. What if we did it in small bites? After several meetings with city officials, Gerald and folks from the central business district team came up with a four-phase development plan for seventeen of the most valuable acres in the district's epicenter. It was a three-way partnership between Armada Hoffler, Gerald and the Beach. We used a special tax designation that had been approved by the state to make the numbers work. Once again, media naysayers and anti-growth foes howled, misrepresenting the tax incentives as a boondoggle. I have to give city officials credit for not caving to the cynics. It was critical that we put on a unified front and educate a more reasonable public about the project. We would be creating jobs and expanding the city's tax base, not draining its coffers or diverting money from schools—a ridiculous but nonetheless persistent notion. Town Center was a huge investment from all of us and we needed to stay focused and positive.

Construction began in 2001. We built an entire downtown in four phases, starting with Armada Hoffler, a twenty-one floor office tower that would become our corporate headquarters. The next phase included luxury apartments and condominiums to get people living downtown, and more parking garages. Phase three was the most ambitious of all—the tallest building in Virginia, a thirty-seven-story Westin Hotel with two hundred thirty-six rooms and one hundred and nineteen condos. I bought the penthouse condo in large part as a visible endorsement of the project. Lou, Russ and others in our company also bought units. The phase also included a performing arts center across the street, just a few steps from the Westin, Virginia's tallest building.

The Armada Hoffler tower filled up quickly with top tenants, including a prestigious law firm, the office of then U.S. Senator George Allen, and a local CBS-affiliate TV station. It was also kind of funny, and certainly ironic, that the very newspaper railing against the project was negotiating with the city to sell its dumpy, mold-infested two-story satellite office, which sat in the middle of our sparkling new downtown.

What probably gave us the single biggest boost was P.F. Chang's. Gerald convinced owners of the highly regarded China bistro to give the Beach a chance. By then, we had lots of office workers and a seven-story Hilton Garden Inn. People needed to eat and entertain. Chang's opened with fanfare and patrons mobbed it. It became the catalyst to attract other equally admired restaurants envious of Chang's sales receipts. We were able to land California Pizza Kitchen, Red Star Tavern, Cold Stone Creamery and a bevy of others. It didn't take long for downtown Virginia Beach to rival downtown Norfolk as a weekend hot spot for entertainment.

The project really couldn't have gone much better. As a company, we invested tens of millions into it. The office and retail space leased quickly at premium rates. Our only significant worry was the condos we still owned in the Westin and across the street in another building. We had sold enough to recover our cost of building them, but we had to pay loans on those that remained unsold.

By late 2006, we began to see the residential real estate market soften. Chatter about a real estate bubble intensified in Washington and on business news talk shows. We had survived two other recessions and knew that, as in the past, the real estate market was overheating. Housing values had increased by a third or more over a very short time. It seemed like just about anyone could get a loan to buy a place. Lenders were giving away cash for houses based on the assumption that home values would keep rising. We started to see the danger signs, just as we had before the commercial real estate bust of the late 1980s and the savings and loan debacle a decade before that. But like just about everyone else, we underestimated the crash of 2007. The Wall Street calamity took out major banks and would nearly push the country into a Great Depression.

When the bottom fell out and the markets crashed, my personal wealth got hammered. Armada Hoffler, however, was on pretty stable ground, at least compared to many other developers and real estate investors. Our experience with two previous recessions taught lessons that I set as rules for the company: We do not speculate on land and only buy it when we need it to build. We do not build unless we have tenants lined up. We have to maintain enough cash flow to sustain us in bad times.

During much of the decade we sat on the sidelines, sometimes to the frustration of people in our company as other developers borrowed easy money from banks and bought up tons of land. Many of them jumped in the game after the federal government closed hundreds of savings and loan banks the previous decade and sold their land holdings for pennies on the dollar. Opportunists flipped the land for profits and kept buying new properties to double down again. The real estate balloon expanded fast and skyrocketed.

The government again was forced to step up and bailout banks that had fueled the bubble, mostly to collect fees for making and processing loans. Fraudulent applications were submitted to get loans and just about anyone could buy property. Banks were offering zero-down-payment loans that required interest-only payments at low rates for the first few years. This "free money" created a gold rush fever for land, houses and other buildings, which was like pumping helium into an already inflated market.

When the bubble burst, everyone got hurt. Real estate values crashed, making properties worth less than the amount owed on them. Wall Street bankers had bundled and sold billions of dollars' worth of these bad loans as investments to the federal government and other banks, ultimately triggering a catastrophic global financial collapse.

Money for real estate projects quickly dried up. Land speculators, some in Virginia Beach, were ruined. No one wanted to buy their land or buildings, and they were out of cash to pay on the loans. Speculators started folding or declaring bankruptcy, sticking the banks they had borrowed from with even more bad debt. It was frightening watching the financial system unravel.

Financing for new development had dried up almost overnight. Fortunately, getting financing wasn't a problem for my company. The bigger issue was the financial health of our clients. The Great Recession, as it has come to be known, scared everyone into being prudent. Our retailers were seeing big drops in business sales, making it difficult to keep up their lease payments. Lou, Russ and the other partners figured it was better to keep retail space filled at lower rents than to have it sit empty. So we renegotiated a lot of leases.

Companies were scared and in survival mode, so no one was expanding or looking for new space. That hurt us too. We met with Beach city officials and mutually agreed to postpone phase four of Town Center. Thankfully, we had good cash flow from other buildings. We had some very large projects underway that would keep our crews busy a couple of years too: an office tower for the prestigious Richmond law firm Williams Mullen; a proton therapy medical building at Hampton University; and a Four Seasons Hotel in Baltimore.

Despite our many projects, partnerships and relatively low debt, the Great Recession continued to batter our clients and industry. The stock market had lost about forty percent of its value, and real estate prices continued to free fall. We had decent cash flow but not enough to carry the entire company. Like just about every other business, we had to cut back. We started with executive pay cuts and by slashing other expenses. As the recession deepened, we were forced to eliminate nearly half of the two hundred jobs in the company.

There were lots of tears and angst. We were forced to dismiss some who had been with us for decades, great people

who had been part of the fabric of the company—mail clerks,
construction site chiefs, property managers, administrative
assistants, marketers. No corner of the operation was untouched.
The atmosphere became very Darwinian. More than once, Russ,
Lou and the partners sat sullen, feeling battered and tired,
wondering if it was time to get out of this topsy-turvy business.
Three recessions will do that to you. But they'll also make you
strong. We knew better times were ahead and began to feel a
hint of optimism when we auctioned off our remaining Westin
tower condos. We had sold eighty-eight of the one hundred
and twenty before the markets crashed and were only able to
sell eight more over the next two years. We decided to try and
unload the rest through bidding. To our amazement, it worked.
There were actually people with cash waiting for bargains. We
sold all sixteen in November 2011, and the prices on some were
bid up close to what we had initially been asking. Lou said that
after the sale, he finally got a good night's sleep for the first time
in months. Our company would survive, yet again and be ready
to catch the next growth wave. That would be our legacy.

CHAPTER XX
Lessons Learned

"In the end, most people ask for something.
Most people get around to it. If you're not careful,
it will make you cynical."

Not long ago, an old pole barn at Point Farm caught fire. The building was set in a remote corner of the property and was used mostly to store mowers, tools and other lawn equipment. Fire trucks came and quickly contained the blaze. No one was hurt; nothing else damaged. A couple of the local TV stations thought this was newsworthy and promptly posted it on their websites. I got a call from someone telling me that I was in the news. I remember thinking: "I'm just a real estate developer, and it's just an old storage building."

I think about the attention I have received, how I often don't want it, don't need it, but how much I love it. It is great to be a standout, to be recognized, to be at the head of line or at least have the ability to move it.

Over the years, I have often thought about how I was placed in the spotlight because of my business successes and connections. I thought about NASCAR driver Kurt Busch, who got married at Point Farm in what was supposed to be a private ceremony, only to have TV news helicopters and newspaper reporters in boats trying to get a look. Then there's my close friend and business partner, NFL Hall of Famer Bruce Smith, who can hardly step out of the office without someone asking for an autograph or a picture or a high-five. I think about Doug Wilder and Mark Warner, friends who endured unrelenting scrutiny in the service of their state and country. These are tough, smart men willing to take a bruising to accomplish what they believe in. I deeply admire their conviction.

I have viewed politicians through the same lens I view everyone else. I size up the person and their actions, not their rhetoric. When it comes to politics, I have found that neither party has all of the solutions or is responsible for all of the problems. Often times, when I was taking measure of an aspiring or sitting elected official, I would meet with my dad. Inevitably, he would remind me to support "the man, not the party," as he has done throughout his life. I have adopted that credo. Even though I was active in the Democratic party because of my friendships with Doug and Mark, I remain a political Independent. Politicians who know me know that I am an equal opportunity campaign contributor. I have supported a broad spectrum that has even included bedrock conservatives like Oliver North, the controversial Iran-Contra figure and former Marine, and a bevy of Republican state lawmakers, city council members and sheriffs. I also have long admired and supported former governor and U.S. Senator George Allen, an unabashed conservative whose social agenda doesn't always jibe with mine, but who has been a man of unyielding integrity. When people ask me why I like George, I tell them the answer is easy: George doesn't have a mean bone in his body. He speaks his mind in an uncalculating, sometimes unrehearsed way, which has gotten him into trouble. I find his candor refreshing.

Not long after George was elected governor, he personally picked up the phone to call to tell me that I would not be reappointed to the University of Virginia Board, a position I had deeply enjoyed. George explained that my seat would be filled with one of his longtime allies and supporters. I told George I was disappointed, but that I also appreciated that he had the class and the respect to call me personally. I was also impressed by his loyalty to his longtime supporter. I still admire and support George.

"The thing with Dan is that you have to earn his support," George says when asked about his relationship with me. Increasingly in Virginia and throughout the country, the key to winning elections is garnering support of Independent voters, George says. "Dan is not the only Independent businessman, but he is a prominent one. He is someone you want to have in your corner. When you get the support of Dan, it means a lot."

More than once during his campaigns for the Senate, George has used me and members of my company as a sounding board for various policy proposals under discussion. I have been very candid with George about my feelings on issues such as the impact of the capital gains tax on the real estate business, for example. If George thinks I am wrong he'll say so, instead of simply telling me what he thinks I want to hear. That's a rare quality.

There is no substitute for loyalty or honesty in any aspect of life. They're about the only things I have demanded from those closest to me or those seeking my support. Loyalty doesn't mean blindly bowing to everything I say or sucking up. But it does mean being honest about feelings and motivations, dealing with disagreements face-to-face and settling them in private. Loyalty is mutual; you have to give it to get it. Once the bond is broken, it's difficult to mend.

It has been heady stuff to have governors return your phone calls and to host famous people at your home. It's also humbling to discover that those with status struggle with many of the same challenges as just about everyone else. Once you drill down through their outer layers of wealth or power or position, you discover that just about all of us want affirmation and respect, we want to be healthy and want our families or loved ones to be safe, happy and successful. Those are the things that bind us, that common thread. Another denominator is having fun, which, unfortunately, eludes too many people.

Most who know me well would say that fun has been one of my specialties. I think they would say that Dan Hoffler has made a lot of money and he knows how to enjoy it. I hope they would say that I have been generous too. Yes, I have made a lot of money, and I have spent a ton. I have shared my fortune in lots of ways for causes or people I believe in. I have helped put dozens of people in business.

Most people don't know that side of me. Detractors see a guy who is flamboyant and ostentatious. George Allen calls me "audacious" because I dream big. I consider that a compliment. The fact is, I have refused to allow negativity to shape me or my lifestyle. I'm also dismissive of those who blame others for their shortcomings, and I have little tolerance for the intolerant.

When it comes to religion and personal lifestyle, I have a laissez faire philosophy. It's much easier and convenient to judge people than to try and understand them. I practice the latter. You have to respect someone enough to respect their opinions and personal beliefs, even if they're different from yours. Intolerant or cruel people step on others or drag them down. I avoid those types.

Am I audacious? Yes. My company and I have dreamed big. Am I flamboyant? Yes. I spend a lot and live large, but I live within my means and my family has been well taken care of. Am I ostentatious? Yes. I have fancy cars, clothes and houses. But does all of that stuff define me? No. Has anyone suffered because of it? No. I never have forgotten who I am or from where I came. I am still a kid from Portsmouth, a guy with fantastic parents who injected me with self-confidence and a positive outlook. Because of them, I seek the good in others and focus on the good in myself.

Hard work is the other part of my DNA. Nothing has been given to me. In my early career and even now in my sixties, I am constantly on airplanes to attend meetings or meet potential clients to seal the next deal. My wife and I continue to host countless parties to bring interesting people together or to get to know someone better. I and my partners at Armada Hoffler still hustle to keep our company healthy and vibrant. We've had far more successes than failures. We've done twenty public-private cost sharing deals that have helped transform skylines and infused cities with vibrancy and growth. We continue to build marquee office towers and hotels, even in a down economy. I am especially proud of my company and Virginia Beach city leaders for having the courage and conviction to thwart naysayers and create an entire downtown. Russ, Lou and I have been extremely fortunate to have a backstop of gifted senior managers, people who have worked diligently and tirelessly to grow our company. Some have been with us for more than thirty years, which I believe is a testament to the loyalty and spirit at Armada Hoffler. Scores of great leaders and workers have contributed to our success, too many to count.

Mine continues to be a go-go life with lots of complexity and lots of reward. Among the achievements I am most proud of and challenged by is serving as a director on the board of a Fortune 500 company. I was invited to join the Shaw Group after meeting its chief executive, James M. Bernhard Jr., on a grouse hunting trip in Spain with my travel buddy and hunting partner Tom Capps. Tom's energy company had been working with Shaw, an engineering, construction and technology behemoth with twenty-nine thousand employees worldwide. Like Tom and I, Jim Bernhard liked wing shooting, so the three of us traveled to Madrid for a red-legged partridge drive, known around the world as the "sport of kings." Jim and I hit it off on that trip. I learned a lot about him and the company he

Jim Bernhard, me and members of The Shaw Group Board of Directors.

built. Shaw, based in Baton Rouge, started in the mid-1980s as a fabrication company that expanded into pipe sales. Jim took the company public in 1994, initiating a series of mergers and acquisitions that morphed Shaw into one of the world's largest designers and builders of manufacturing centers and power plants. By 2003, Shaw made Fortune magazine's list of the five hundred largest companies. I was honored to join the Shaw board as an independent director in 2006, serving with highly accomplished executives of other major U.S. companies. Through Shaw, I have gained an international perspective on business and government. The company's dealings are massive and its leadership well-honed. Jim is absolutely brilliant to watch in action.

In addition to my pride in what I have learned in business, I am proud of what I have accomplished personally and who I have become. And I am just as proud of my four children. I see in each of them many of the qualities that my parents instilled in me. My kids are respectful of others, independent-minded, and loving and loyal to me and each other. We like each other's company and hanging out together—at least I like to think so. My oldest daughter, Sara, has given me two beautiful grandchildren, David Vines and Wyatt, and she's a terrific, dedicated mother. She has a warm heart and compassionate spirit. I see a lot of myself in my second daughter, Kristy, who has my mother's fiery spirit and who is the life of a party. She warms quickly to others and loves telling stories. My oldest son, Daniel, who was born on the fourth of July, has grown into a charming, college-bound young man with a quick wit and ease around others. Like his dad, he loves the outdoors and trading gentle barbs with me when we tease each other. The youngest of my four, Hunter, has a sweetness and calm that reminds me of my dad. He can sit for hours tying intricate tiny flies that he uses for catching trout on a fly rod. In 2011, he became the National Youth Fly Fishing Champion and is featured in an instructional video of the sport. My boys and I have traveled a lot together, spending countless days hunting and fishing or just being friends. My children are my greatest fortune. No boy or man could ask for a better sister than my beloved Sharon. She has always looked out for me and our parents, providing the entire Hoffler family with relentless devotion and support

As I have said earlier in these pages, I have had some luck in my career and a group of very loyal and very talented business partners. I have also had the pleasure of bonding with some very smart and influential political and business leaders over four decades. But these successes and connections didn't just fall randomly from above. I have worked very hard at getting to know others and learning from them. The travel and networking has been fun and enjoyable, but it has been exhausting too. There have been many weekends when I wished for some quiet time instead of packing for my next trip or rising on a frigid morning before sunrise to take an associate or friend on a duck hunt.

My daughter Kristy tells a story about one of her girlfriends who brought her young child to Point Farm for a visit. Kristy was showing them the main house, which the little girl assumed belonged to Kristy. The little girl said, "You must work really hard to have a house like this." Kristy said, "No, honey, this is my daddy's house," to which the little girl responded, "Then your daddy must work really hard."

That's how I would like to be remembered—as the guy who worked really hard for his success and then shared his good fortune with others. I also hope that others will remember me as someone who, with hard work and a positive outlook, overachieved. Some people are blessed with genius, artistic prodigy, or born into money or power. None of this was true of me. I was a fairly average kid who dreamed big as a young man. My parents gave me the confidence and support to believe in myself. Thankfully, I had the energy to keep motoring, even in hard times. I took some big risks and got lucky a few times. But luck and risks really are just opportunities that we make for ourselves. You have to be in the right place at the right time for "place" and "time" to work in your favor. And when you don't get it right, don't be afraid to move on. I've done that in both my personal and business lives. Worse than making a mistake is getting trapped or defined by one.

My life, just as that of my company's, has evolved in phases. I think we shift from being young and idealistic to pragmatic, then to seasoned, then to wise. Perhaps in this phase of my life, I am returning more to idealism as I contemplate my legacy. This